TAROT Lovers' "LITTLE" BLACK BOOK
of Tarot Card Meanings

Karyn Easton

4880 Lower Valley Road • Atglen, PA 19310

Other Schiffer Books By The Author:

Tarot, Birth Cards, and You: Keys to Empowering Yourself
by Bonnie Cehovet, Illustrated by Karyn Easton
978-0-7643-3902-8 $19.99

Copyright © 2012 by Karyn Easton
Library of Congress Control Number: 2012953219

    All rights reserved. No part of this work may be reproduced or used in any form or by any means — graphic, electronic, or mechanical, including photocopying or information storage and retrieval systems — without written permission from the publisher.
    The scanning, uploading and distribution of this book or any part thereof via the Internet or via any other means without the permission of the publisher is illegal and punishable by law. Please purchase only authorized editions and do not participate in or encourage the electronic piracy of copyrighted materials.
    "Schiffer," "Schiffer Publishing, Ltd. & Design," and the "Design of pen and inkwell" are registered trademarks of Schiffer Publishing, Ltd.

Designed by Justin Watkinson
Type set in Bookman Old Style/Book Antiqua

ISBN: 978-0-7643-4133-5
Printed in China

Schiffer Books are available at special discounts for bulk purchases for sales promotions or premiums. Special editions, including personalized covers, corporate imprints, and excerpts can be created in large quantities for special needs. For more information contact the publisher:

Published by Schiffer Publishing, Ltd.
4880 Lower Valley Road
Atglen, PA 19310
Phone: (610) 593-1777; Fax: (610) 593-2002
E-mail: Info@schifferbooks.com

For the largest selection of fine reference books on this and related subjects, please visit our website at
www.schifferbooks.com
We are always looking for people to write books on new and related subjects. If you have an idea for a book, please contact us at
proposals@schifferbooks.com

This book may be purchased from the publisher.
Please try your bookstore first.
You may write for a free catalog.

In Europe, Schiffer books are distributed by
Bushwood Books
6 Marksbury Ave.
Kew Gardens
Surrey TW9 4JF England
Phone: 44 (0) 20 8392 8585; Fax: 44 (0) 20 8392 9876
E-mail: info@bushwoodbooks.co.uk
Website: www.bushwoodbooks.co.uk

About the Author/Artist

Karyn Easton achieved a 1st Class Honors Degree in Industrial Design Marketing and has worked in the design industry for many years. She lives in Devon in the UK where she concentrates on designing and writing for: www.paranormality.com and www.tarot-lovers.com.

Dedication

This Book is dedicated to my family:

Sylvia, Andrew, Lara, Jamie, Tamzin;
and also to my Dad,
sadly gone, but never forgotten.

Acknowledgments

Many thanks to my family who have supported me throughout both the writing and illustration of this guide. A huge thank you goes out to Richard Ward-Smith of www.tangramdesign.co.uk for all of his beautiful design work at *Tarot Lovers*. Many thanks to my friends: Sheila, Chris, Debby, Jean, and Betty for providing a wonderful Tarot circle in which to learn more about the cards. And finally, many thanks to Bonnie Cehovet, who not only encouraged me through her very positive reviews of my work (http://bonniecehovet.wordpress.com/), she also believed in my deck enough to include it in her excellent work on *Tarot Birth Cards: Tarot Birth Cards and You*.

Contents

Introduction 7

The Major Arcana
0 The Fool. 8
I The Magician. 10
II The Papess 12
III The Empress 15
IV The Emperor. 18
V The Pope. 20
VI The Lovers 23
VII The Chariot 26
VIII Strength 29
IX The Hermit 32
X Wheel of Fortune. . . . 35
XI Justice. 37
XII The Hanged Man . . . 40
XIII Death 43
XIV Temperance 46
XV The Devil 49
XVI The Tower 52
XVII The Star 55
XVIII The Moon 57
XIX The Sun. 60
XX Judgement 63
XXI The World. 66

Wands
Ace Wands. 68
II Wands. 70
III Wands 72
IV Wands 74
V Wands. 76
VI Wands 78
VII Wands 80
VIII Wands. 83
IX Wands 85
X Wands. 87
Page Wands. 90
Knight Wands 92
Queen Wands 94
King Wands. 97

Cups
Ace Cups 100
II Cups 102
III Cups. 104
IV Cups. 106
V Cups 108
VI Cups. 110
VII Cups 113
VIII Cups 115
IX Cups. 117
X Cups 119
Page Cups 122
Knight Cups. 124
Queen Cups. 127
King Cups 130

Swords

- Ace Swords 133
- II Swords 135
- III Swords 137
- IV Swords 139
- V Swords 141
- VI Swords 143
- VII Swords 145
- VIII Swords 147
- IX Swords 149
- X Swords 152
- Page Swords 154
- Knight Swords 157
- Queen Swords 160
- King Swords 163

Coins

- Ace Coins 166
- II Coins 169
- III Coins 172
- IV Coins 174
- V Coins 177
- VI Coins 180
- VII Coins 182
- VIII Coins 184
- IX Coins 187
- X Coins 189
- Page Coins 192
- Knight Coins 195
- Queen Coins 198
- King Coins 201

Additional Notes 204

Bibliography 207

"When the wheel spins around, luck and fortune can be found."

Introduction

The Tarot Lovers' "Little" Black Book of Tarot Meanings is intended to be a useful resource for anyone learning the traditional meanings of Tarot cards. It contains key information relating to each card in an easy-to-use format, making it an ideal choice for both beginners and professionals alike. The meanings are based on the traditional meanings of the cards and relate to a standard 78-card deck. Both the upright positions of the cards and the reversed positions of the cards are covered. The meanings are also suitable for both *Rider-Waite* and *Tarot de Marseilles* style decks. *Tarot Lovers' "Little" Black Book of Tarot Meanings* is an essential, concise reference source for anyone interested in Tarot.

0 The Fool

The Fool (Le Fou)
The Spirit of the Aether

CARD NUMBER	0
KEY NUMBER	11
RULERSHIP	Air
HEBREW LETTER	Aleph
TRANSLATION	Ox
NUMERICAL VALUE	3
ASTROLOGICAL ASSOCIATIONS	Pluto/Uranus (Modern)
CANDLE	White
CRYSTAL	Orange Carnelian

Guideline Divinatory Meanings:

Keywords (Upright): Moving onwards and upwards, achievement, attainment, success

Upright – Beginnings, most probably of journeys which may be possibly mental, physical or spiritual. The beginning of a new life-cycle. Energy, force, happiness, and optimism. The overturning of the status quo or existing states by unexpected happenings. Innocence, naivety, and spontaneity. Important decisions to be made.

The Fool card is indicative that you could be about to embark upon something totally new. This could take the form of a journey that was not planned. This journey does not necessarily mean that you are going somewhere; it could be a journey of the mind. Either way, you are going to be starting a new cycle and this is a really exciting time for you. You will be filled with renewed energy and you will have a sense of optimism and spontaneity. Any journey of self discovery that you may take will be filled with optimism and enjoyment. There may be some uncertainties arising in your life but this will bring forth many opportunities that could lead to bigger and better things. Old ways have now been cast aside and the familiar replaced with the unfamiliar. You may also find that you will have many decisions to make along the way. An interesting path lies ahead for you, but you must trust your judgment along the way.

- Follow your head as well as your heart and make sure all's in place before you depart

Keywords (Reversed): Frustration, distrust, fear of change, application of willpower

Ill Dignified or Reversed – Ill-advised risks, impulsive action, choices and rash decisions. Foolishness, gambling, instability, and the wasting or frittering away of creative energy. A bad time for commitments and can be an indication of someone who starts many new things but never finishes them. They may also consistently seek changes in their environment or job.

The Fool card reversed is a card that advises against any unnecessary risks and warns against carelessness at this time. Now is not the time to be taking any ill-advised risks or making any hasty decisions. It is a good time, however, to channel your energy much more positively and creatively and to stop any time wasting. There may be someone around you who is having difficulty in acting on their intuition and in some respects may even be trying to shirk their responsibilities. If this person is a work colleague, then they may be the type of person to do the minimum required, which sometimes may be problematic. If you are considering any serious commitments, then this card suggests that you should weigh up everything very carefully before jumping in.

- Feeling blocked, nothing to say, stay true to your dreams and get back on your way

I The Magician

The Magician (Le Bateleur)
The Magnus of Power

CARD NUMBER	1
KEY NUMBER	12
RULERSHIP	Mercury
HEBREW LETTER	Beth
TRANSLATION	House
NUMERICAL VALUE	9
ASTROLOGICAL ASSOCIATIONS	Mercury
CANDLE	Yellow
CRYSTAL	Topaz

Guideline Divinatory Meanings:

Keywords (Upright): Drive and determination, ambition, self motivation

Upright – Mastery of the material world, creative action, self discipline and a willingness to take risks. An ability to recognise one's own potential, the power to initiate, communication and wit.

The Magician card is symbolic of things being revealed just like a magician pulls a rabbit from his hat. It is a card that is linked to the infinite power of the universe and a lot of emphasis is placed upon mastery, skill, and power. This is a card of initiation and communication and mastering the circumstances that present themselves. If you are starting something new, then this is the card for you, as it often represents the determination and initiative needed to succeed at things. This success could be either spiritual or material, but either way The Magician is a good omen.

- When feelings might be running low, The Magician is there to help things flow

Keywords (Reversed): Confusion, hesitation, lack of energy, giving in easily, poor self image

Ill Dignified or Reversed – Confusion, hesitation, inability to make decisive choices. Inability to properly utilise time or talents. Lack of inspiration or energy. Giving up easily, poor self image, poor coordination and sometimes difficulties learning.

The Magician reversed is an odd character; when he turns upside down, his tools fall off his table and his genuine magic is gone. This is someone now who figuratively turns from a doctor into a quack, or a salesman into a trickster, because the genuine tools of the trade have gone. Now is the time to ensure that people and situations are exactly what they seem. When this card reversed shows up in a spread, try to guard against any confusion in situations. Steer clear of any "dodgy dealings" right now. Lack of energy and a poor self image will not help at this time. When you come across The Magician who's fallen upside down, help him up, give him his tools, and tell him he can be good again. With his tools all bent he is no real use to you now.

- Lack of help and hidden things, may hinder progress in the wings.

II The Papess

The High Priestess or Papess (La Papesse)
The Priestess of the Silver Star

CARD NUMBER	2
KEY NUMBER	13
RULERSHIP	The Moon
HEBREW LETTER	Gimel
TRANSLATION	Camel
NUMERICAL VALUE	9
ASTROLOGICAL ASSOCIATIONS	Virgo
CANDLE	Lavender
CRYSTAL	Opal

Guideline Divinatory Meanings:

Keywords (Upright): Intuitive insights, deep knowledge, mysteries revealed, imagination, psychic and artistic ability

Upright – Intuition, wisdom, and secret knowledge, the feminine side of the male personality. Something remains yet to be revealed, but patience must be observed. Duality and mystery. Hidden influences affect both home and work, and intuitive insight suggests new solutions. The influence of women.

The Papess (The High Priestess) is generally a good card if you are looking or searching for something that remains hidden, because this is a card that represents the bringing forth of hidden knowledge and wisdom. Sometimes when she appears in a spread you may discover a secret that you never expected to learn. This hidden knowledge will certainly be to your advantage as it is the job of The Papess to ensure that you have all of the information required to continue along your chosen path. A card of intuition and psychic ability, you may also find that her presence in your reading indicates information imparted to you by less conventional means, for example you may find that, at this time, your hunches prove to be right, and you are highly intuitive at present. Any knowledge or wisdom may not become instantly clear, but as long as you are patient, then all will be revealed to you in the end.

- Hidden things not yet revealed. Until the time's right, they'll stay tightly sealed.
- The "Mystery" card.

Keywords (Reversed): Lack of foresight, ignorance of facts, things not what they seem, the suppressed feminine side

Ill Dignified or Reversed – Lack of personal harmony and problems resulting from a lack of foresight. Suppression of the feminine or intuitive side of the personality. Facile and surface knowledge. Repression and ignorance of true facts and feelings. In women, an inability to come to terms with other women or themselves. Things and circumstances are not what they seem.

The Papess (The High Priestess) reversed is a card that is indicative of something that remains hidden and will not necessarily be revealed. Unlike her upright counterpart, The Papess in the reversed position is the keeper of secrets, someone who is not waiting for the right moment to share them. When she turns upside down, her book slams shut and she lands on top. All she knows, is now locked inside. This could be a time that you need to pay attention to your intuition as things may not always be as they seem. For a man, The Papess can be seen as one aspect of the feminine element within man, the Anima. However, when she is reversed in a man's spread, this could indicate the negative effects on him by a woman or women. Sometimes this card reversed can point to a lack of inner knowledge, so the advice here would be to tread a well-known path and listen to your inner voice. The Papess reversed is not a lady who will willingly give up her knowledge to help. Try to keep optimistic and trust your own inner voice and, more importantly, try to establish all of the facts. Pry open her book and all will be revealed.

- Many secrets are to remain hidden. These are truths that are strictly forbidden.

III The Empress

The Empress (L'Imperatrice)
The Daughter of the Mighty Ones

CARD NUMBER	3
KEY NUMBER	14
RULERSHIP	Venus
HEBREW LETTER	Daleth
TRANSLATION	Door
NUMERICAL VALUE	9
ASTROLOGICAL ASSOCIATIONS	Libra
CANDLE	Pink
CRYSTAL	Tourmaline

Guideline Divinatory Meanings:

Keywords (Upright): Well-being, stability, balance, harmony, prosperity

Upright – The promotion of well-being and security. Creativeness in financial affairs, love, and parenthood. Maternal care, domestic stability, abundance, and material wealth. Fertility, security, achievement of goals, and growth. Depending on surrounding cards, sometimes marriage and pregnancy.

THE MAJOR ARCANA

The Empress card is one of maternal instincts, fertility, growth, and domestic bliss. However, this fertility is not necessarily just in terms of human pregnancy. Indeed, this card, symbolic of nurturing, can mean the nurturing of a wide variety of things; for example: a new venture, business idea, new romance, new relationships, and anything that takes the form of being created and grown. It can also signify that you have a strong desire to have love and affection in your life. Although the card is symbolic of pregnancy, in a business sense this card can suggest some level of home working and the success of upcoming projects. Therefore, if you are embarking upon something new, The Empress card is a really good card for you. In a relationship sense, The Empress indicates a partnership or union within which both partners are happy. You are entering a fertile period of your life in both a creative and spiritual sense. Early cards showed The Empress as a pregnant lady and the card can sometimes mean marriage, pregnancy, births, and prosperity, but it is possibly better to think of The Empress card as the archetypal mother who helps to look after the querent's affairs. In a man's spread, The Empress tends to represent his nearest and dearest and a love of infinite proportions.

- Now is a time of harmony and bliss, life is great, nothing's amiss.
- The "Pregnancy" card.

Keywords (Reversed): Domestic and relationship issues, paucity, unbalanced activity, separation of ties, fertility issues

   Ill Dignified or Reversed – Possible domestic problems, financial issues, lack of affection and achievement. Creative blocks and possible problems with a relationship. Issues that may relate to fertility, sterility, promiscuity, and pregnancy.

The Empress card reversed truly is a card turned on its head. Instead of being an archetypal mother figure that is seen to nurture everyone and everything, this "Mother Earth" in her reversed position is something more of a wicked stepmother. Her maternal instincts have abandoned her as she in turn has abandoned her nurturing nature. In her upside down state she is in a completely disturbed environment and unable to grow anything in her garden. When she presents upside down in a spread don't expect your creative juices to flow; this may be a time of creative blocks. In a relationship, it may be a time that both partners need to give and take a little more. Pregnancy and fertility are not well starred when she is around. In the extreme sense she can also present as quite a destructive card that wants to spoil that which has already been created or achieved. For this reason, when this feisty lady turns up, watch out for arguments with partners, friends, or lovers; guard against any insecurities, try and get your creative juices flowing again, and above all, don't neglect things that need attention.

- A time of planting but nothing to grow; life could be better and this you know.

Hidden Meaning: The Empress, together with the Eight of Cups may signify problems with a mother, mother figure, or mother in law.

IV The Emperor

The Emperor (L'Empereur)
Son of the Morning; Chief Among the Mighty

CARD NUMBER	4
KEY NUMBER	15
RULERSHIP	Aries
HEBREW LETTER	Heh
TRANSLATION	Window
NUMERICAL VALUE	12
ASTROLOGICAL ASSOCIATIONS	Scorpio
CANDLE	Dark Blue
CRYSTAL	Red Carnelian

Guideline Divinatory Meanings:

Keywords (Upright): Power, authority, self discipline, stability

Upright – Competitiveness, forcefulness in development and execution. Authority, structure, governmental and corporate identities. Worldly power, self control gained through experience. Ability to shoulder responsibility. Powerful individuals, ambition together with the possibility of long-term achievement.

The Emperor is a very paternal card; he can often represent a father figure or a boss who is ready and able to help with any obstacles in your life, but only as long as you take a very pragmatic approach to any obstacles you may face. The Emperor also stands for achievement and the pinnacle of knowledge and higher attainment. But either way, The Emperor is there to help you with your business and/or personal affairs. This is a good card to have, particularly if you have any issues in your life at the moment that may need sorting out, but be ready to make all of the necessary changes and be prepared to act instantly.

- With gifts at hand, armed and ready, help is around to keep you steady.

Keywords (Reversed): Dislike of authority, immaturity, manipulation, inability to govern weakness

Ill Dignified or Reversed – Loss or dislike of authority, corporate, governmental, or parental. Immaturity and indecision. Weakness, manipulative friends or colleagues.

The Emperor card reversed, just like his counterpart The Empress, seems to become a completely different character when inverted. When he is turned upside down, his crown falls to the floor and his throne comes crashing down with it, hopelessly denting his ability to rule – just in the same way that The Empress' throne breaks up her garden and stifles her ability to nurture and grow things. A king without a crown or a throne would find it very difficult to rule or command the authority required to maintain his reign. In this state, The Emperor reversed can become either completely self obsessed and tyrannical, or he can head for the exit and shy away from his usual duties. When he turns up in your spread, it could mean that you are encountering difficulties with a strong male figure who could be either a boss, parent, or partner. The best advice here is to try to avoid any unnecessary conflicts. If you have any decisions to be made or any responsibilities to be undertaken, then approach them with maturity. Don't try to be too rebellious at this time and try not to shirk any responsibilities. If it is responsibility that you crave, try not to be too disappointed if it doesn't quite happen for you this time. In a relationship, The Emperor reversed can indicate that there has been a lack of commitment lately from a partner. It can also signify in a relationship that the woman is becoming more of a mother figure than a wife.

- With sword at hand, ready to drop, keep working hard, or face the chop.

V The Pope

The Pope (Le Pape)
The Magnus of the Eternal

CARD NUMBER	5
KEY NUMBER	16
RULERSHIP	Taurus
HEBREW LETTER	Vau
TRANSLATION	Nail
NUMERICAL VALUE	12
ASTROLOGICAL ASSOCIATIONS	Jupiter
CANDLE	Purple
CRYSTAL	Rose Quartz

Guideline Divinatory Meanings:

Keywords (Upright): Religious guidance, traditional teacher, wise mentor, wisdom, truth, spirituality

Upright – Ritual and routine, religious guidance and authority, education in its formal sense. A seeker after knowledge and wisdom. Good sound advice, teaching, and constructive counsel. Marriage, partnerships, and morality.

The Pope or Hierophant signifies advice coming in the form of a wise, traditional and conventional teacher. He stands for conventional wisdom and spirituality that he teaches through the workings of your inner self or psyche. In terms of where this wisdom may come from, The Pope represents a very pious and kind person. For example, but not limited to: a favorite uncle, teacher, rabbi, or clergyman. Certainly, if you have any problems at the moment, then this is the card of help, to enable you to make the correct choices in life, as it is the card of a mentor, spiritual advisor, and practical instructor. He is someone who brings "The wisdom of the heavens down to earth." Depending upon circumstances, this card may sometimes indicate marriage and partnerships which are well starred, if this is what is currently on your mind. However, in this sense, you must beware of putting pressure on your partner and make sure that you are not trying to live up to any unrealistic expectations that they may have of you. In a jovial sense, the phrase to sum up this card might be "Never fear, the Pope (Hierophant) is here."

- The best advice is coming your way. Knowledge and wisdom to brighten your day.
- The "Mentorship" card.

Keywords (Reversed): Dubious advice, gossip, untruths, avoid overindulgence, materialism bars progress

Ill Dignified or Reversed – Misleading or dubious advice, poor counsel, slander, and propaganda. Beware of first impressions. Distortion of truth and possibly a bad time for signing agreements. Misleading advertisements. Unconventionality and rejection of family values.

The Pope or Hierophant reversed is the essence of spiritual leadership gone wrong. In his upright position, The Pope is the embodiment of the highest form of mentorship, yet turned around, he becomes synonymous with religious dogma and single-mindedness. In his reversed position, his guidance comes not from Heaven above, but from the earth below. He could certainly benefit from the advice of: "Let he who is without sin cast the first stone." Upside down, this card represents a man who has become bigoted in his views and very narrow minded. His advice serves his own ends and fulfills his desires, not necessarily those who seek his advice. For this reason when this card turns up reversed in your spread, the advice is to try to guard against distortions of the truth and any poor advice or nasty gossip. In a relationship this card may indicate that both partners are setting out unrealistic expectations of one another, which may be proving difficult. The advice here would be to lower the bar and appreciate what the relationship has to offer, as opposed to what it does not. On the whole, when The Pope reversed card is around, look to thinking "outside of the box" and broaden your horizons, as this will help you to establish the whole picture and not only just the small part someone may want you to see.

- When teaching turns to preaching, and things remain undone, seek out the truth in people, and then you will have won.

Hidden Meaning: The Pope, together with the Two of Cups, can signify marriage to a secure and stable person and a blessing on a marriage.

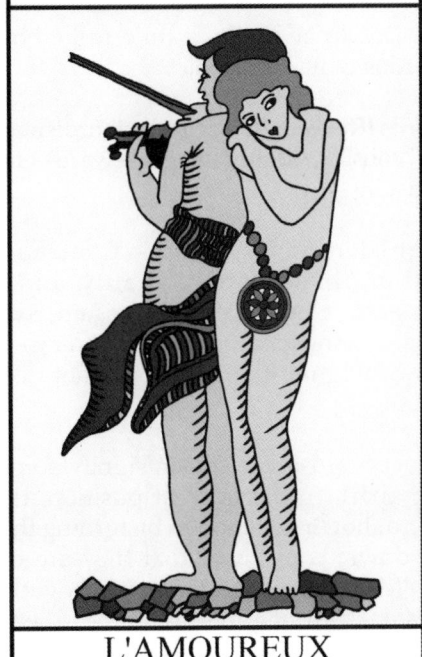

VI The Lovers

The Lovers (L'Amoureux)
The Children of the Voice
The Oracle of the Mighty Gods

CARD NUMBER	6
KEY NUMBER	17
RULERSHIP	Gemini
HEBREW LETTER	Zain
TRANSLATION	Weapon or Sword
NUMERICAL VALUE	12
ASTROLOGICAL ASSOCIATIONS	Venus
CANDLE	Green
CRYSTAL	Citrine

Guideline Divinatory Meanings:

Keywords (Upright): Determination, attraction, magnetism, intuition, choices

Upright – Harmony and union, choices to be made using intuition and not intellect. Difficult decisions to be made, not necessarily about love. Some form of test and consideration about commitments. Abstract thought, internal harmony and union, second sight. Possibly a struggle between two paths.

The Lovers is a card all about love. Not a shallow love but a very deep intense love, and one that you cannot really do without. It could be a new job, a new house, car, item, pet, or person that will suddenly appear in your life, but once you have found that love, you will most certainly not want him, her, or it to leave. If you already have an established relationship, then this card signifies that any obstacles will be overcome in your search for balance, romance, and harmony within that union. In terms of a new relationship, The Lovers card suggests that this new romantic opportunity could be a success. This card is also symbolic of something or someone entirely new entering your life. Once this event has happened, your new set of circumstances may present you with a variety of choices and ultimately may lead to you having to choose between a series of options. Within the context of career, this card suggests that you may have outgrown your old role or job position and, if it is the appropriate time, then maybe you should move onto something new. Although the choice to be made may prove initially hard to make, this is a card of second sight and intuition and is sure to help you in your quest for true love.

- Choices to be made, a time to be bold, the reasons why will unfold.

Keywords (Reversed): Contradiction, disharmony, internal conflict, fidelity issues, beware of making big decisions

Ill Dignified or Reversed – Contradiction, deception, disharmony, duality and one's own internal conflict. Infidelity and romantic disturbances. Indecisiveness, postponing choices, and a warning not to make important decisions at this time.

The Lovers card reversed can signify something coming apart. In the upright position, the two lovers are shown together, so by turning this card upside down, could it be that they are coming apart? Maybe they no longer fit together, or perhaps one is trying to fit with the other, but it just doesn't quite work? If the card in its upright position is all about unity, love, and bonding, then this is a card of opposites when reversed.

For this reason, the simplest message here is one of breakup. However, this could be a breakup in many senses; for example: a family breakup, the breakup of an organization, or the breakup of communications. With all of this in mind, the advice here is to choose your path carefully. Do not make any decisions lightly. Watch out for any relationship difficulties and keep your sense of scruples and morals, especially if strong temptation is put in your path. Sometimes it is not always possible to have the best of both worlds and decisions that lead you to obtaining that goal may not be wise.

- If you feel the choice was wrong, pick yourself up and carry on.

VII The Chariot

The Chariot (Le Chariot)
The Child of the Powers of the Waters
The Lord of the Triumph of Light

CARD NUMBER	7
KEY NUMBER	18
RULERSHIP	Cancer
HEBREW LETTER	Cheth
TRANSLATION	Fenced or Enclosed Field
NUMERICAL VALUE	12
ASTROLOGICAL ASSOCIATIONS	Sagittarius
CANDLE	Bright Red
CRYSTAL	Moonstone

Guideline Divinatory Meanings:

Keywords (Upright): Moving forwards, onwards, and upwards

Upright – Triumph over adversity, overcoming life's obstacles, decisiveness and ambition in achieving one's goals, well-deserved victory. A period of struggle ending in worldly success. Self control, effort, perseverance. Working within the boundaries of one's life to build up a successful existence.

The Chariot is a card about overcoming conflicts and moving forward in a positive direction. These conflicts could be internal or external. Internally, it is a case of ridding yourself of your demons if you have any. Externally, it is a case of managing any conflicting circumstances, people, or events and turning everything to your advantage. The Chariot is there to help speed you onwards and upwards and this is a good card to have in your spread. It can be symbolic of drive, motivation, determination, and is linked to providing the tools necessary for you to win. In a practical sense, it sometimes foretells of a journey by car. However, it must be stressed that although the victory may have already been won, or is about to be won, this is only the start of the journey and you will need to conserve your energy for what may lie ahead. However, The Chariot is generally a good omen and you must put all of your efforts into making your dreams come true.

- If you feel life's an upward hike, what's needed right now is to hop on your bike.

Keywords (Reversed): Disregard for others, envy, avarice, imbalance

Ill Dignified or Reversed – A disregard for others, envy, avarice. Loss of control and chaos in one's personal life, possibly due to personal flaws. Imbalance. Conclusion. A warning against overwhelming ambition and high expectations. The continuation of outdated ideas and traditions.

The Chariot card reversed is a card of standstill. Unlike its upright version, this is a reversed card indicative of lack of movement. Any figurative movement that may come from this card will be both out of control and without direction. Indeed, it is the complete opposite of The Chariot in its upright position. Instead of being able to forge ahead with decisiveness and ambition, The Chariot reversed can be likened to a vehicle that has broken down; and instead of journeys being starred, this is a path littered with problems and blockages. If you imagine The Chariot turned upside down with its wheels spinning wildly in the air, then you know that something caused it to be there.

Speaking metaphorically, could this have been due to loss of control, a collision, an accident, or simply taking a bend too sharply. The advice for anyone who gets this card reversed is to try to take back control of one's life. Until you build up momentum and restore balance, then you are most definitely stuck. In order to move forward again, you need to try to get rid of any feelings of frustration and negative emotions. In a relationship, it may be that one partner wants to move things forward too quickly for the other one and a period of reflection is needed before things get back on track. Take back the reins and restore momentum.

- If you feel life's not on track, change direction and don't look back.
- A card of engine trouble.

Hidden Meaning: The Chariot, together with an Ace, can signify moving and travel.

VIII Strength

Strength (La Force)
The Daughter of the Flaming Sword

CARD NUMBER	8
KEY NUMBER	19
RULERSHIP	Leo
HEBREW LETTER	Teth
TRANSLATION	Serpent
NUMERICAL VALUE	12
ASTROLOGICAL ASSOCIATIONS	Capricorn
CANDLE	Dark Red
CRYSTAL	Tiger's Eye

Guideline Divinatory Meanings:

Keywords (Upright): Rising to the challenge, overcoming obstacles, being in charge of one's inner emotions, self control

Upright – Courage. Self control. The virtue of fortitude. The power of love. Control of passion against one's baser instincts. Determination. Strength and power under control. Energy. Optimism. Generosity, resolve, and reconciliation.

The Strength card is one of self control, willpower, strength of character, and maintaining nerves of steel in any difficult situation. It is a card that represents mastery of an awkward situation and the overcoming of any negative thoughts, instincts, or obstacles. In order to move forward, you will need a huge amount of drive and determination, and as long as you can accept this, then you will be able to succeed. In the process of this success, onlookers will respect you for seeing through the courage of your convictions. Try to think of the Strength card in terms of fire. At first, man was burned by fire and then he learned how to control it, but he never ever lost his respect for its destructive power. In this sense, you are mastering situations, circumstances, and events, and if at any time you have got your fingers burned, you will have learned from the experience and ensure this does not happen again in the future. Where this card is related to a relationship, then communication is the watchword and the ability to listen to one another will help your relationship to grow.

- Strength and love is all you need, to overcome and succeed.

Keywords (Reversed): Power wrongly used, curb the urge to dictate, exchanges with superiors, lack of will, inadequacy, pessimism

Ill Dignified or Reversed – Power wrongly used. Defeat. Lack of willpower. Feelings of inadequacy. Pessimism. Surrender to unworthy impulses. Autocracy. Concession. Inability to act.

The Strength card reversed is a complete opposite to its upright self. In traditional symbolism, the Strength card is depicted with a maiden gently stroking a lion. It could even be said that she is taming that lion. Imagine if that card was literally turned on its head; then the poor maiden would end up with a lion on top of her. In the *Tarot Lovers Tarot* she would end up with two lions on her head! It would seem that something that was well under control is no longer. Indeed a complete turnaround seems to have happened, where the lions, or the situations, that were once contained are now "ruling the roost." For this reason, when this card reversed turns up in your spread, it can mean that something that was once well contained is becoming too big to handle. It may be time to ask for help with a project or situation. Other meanings that are associated with this card include cowardice, weakness, and lack of backbone. If there is any person, situation, or set of circumstances that are becoming difficult, then it is important to re-direct one's inner energies so that progress can be made. Try to avoid situations where a lot of willpower is required. For example, if you are trying to give up smoking, avoid situations that make your goal difficult to achieve, and if it becomes so difficult, then maybe ask for help.

- Some situations you just can't tame, it's not your fault and there's nothing to blame.

IX The Hermit

The Hermit (L'Ermite)
The Prophet of the Eternal
The Magnus of the Voice of Power

CARD NUMBER	9
KEY NUMBER	20
RULERSHIP	Virgo
HEBREW LETTER	Yod
TRANSLATION	The Human Hand Closed to Grasp or Hold
NUMERICAL VALUE	12
ASTROLOGICAL ASSOCIATIONS	Aquarius
CANDLE	Silver
CRYSTAL	Peridot

Guideline Divinatory Meanings:

Keywords (Upright): Introspection, inner reflection, inner calm, soul searching, the inner self

Upright – Caution. Discretion. Need for prudence. Counsel sought and taken. Inner calm. A need to reach into one's inner resources. Assimilation. Planning. A wise guide or spiritual mentor. A time to stand back and reflect upon circumstances.

The Hermit card is symbolic of a time to take stock and to reflect. By having this card in your spread, it could mean that you need to retreat away from all of the general hustle and bustle of life. You may need and want to take some time out to discover your inner peace and wisdom and decide what is really important to you. This card is one of enlightenment and connections and sometimes a desire to simply be just on your own, alone, and away from it all. At present, you may be feeling somewhat fed up with your situation, but after a short period of withdrawal from it all, you will emerge a much wiser and enlightened individual. As well as relating to you, this card can also be indicative of someone entering your life who will serve as a spiritual or physical mentor, who will help you to overcome whatever may be bothering you. Recent difficulties may have left you with feelings of isolation and loneliness, but once you have taken some time out and put past problems behind you, then you will be able to move on in a much more positive direction. The Hermit card is one of success through inner wisdom, reflection and spirituality.

- Watch out for the candle in the dark; this will help you to regain your spark.

Keywords (Reversed): Refusal of counsel or assistance, select associates wisely, immaturity, isolation, bad habits, suspicions

Ill Dignified or Reversed – Refusal of counsel or assistance. Immaturity. Isolation from others. A negative resistance towards help. Groundless suspicions about the motives of others. Imprudent actions or decisions. The continuation of bad habits or unproductive lifestyles. Foolish obstinacy. The reliance on one's own resources that are inadequate.

The Hermit card reversed is all about being in the dark. Upside down, The Hermit completely loses his light, both his inner light and his exterior light. Whereas the card upright is one of enlightenment, the card reversed is more about being in the dark. As a person, The Hermit reversed is someone who can be likened to a bitter unhelpful old man, who uses his self-enforced isolation to formulate not the nicest of plans. He would not be very forthcoming regarding helpful advice; indeed, his advice would probably be questionable at best. This card warns against having a closed mind, against working long hours on your own, and against rejecting good advice from friends and family. Sometimes self reliance is a good thing, but with The Hermit reversed, it may be time to become less obstinate and take help when it is offered. Try to step out from the shadows and into the light and find a way of re-lighting your fire.

- When the candle shines, bask in its light, as this will help you with any plight.

X Wheel of Fortune

Wheel of Fortune (La Roue de Fortune)
The Lord of the Forces of Life

CARD NUMBER	10
KEY NUMBER	21
RULERSHIP	Jupiter
HEBREW LETTER	Kaph
TRANSLATION	Hand
NUMERICAL VALUE	9
ASTROLOGICAL ASSOCIATIONS	Uranus
CANDLE	Orange
CRYSTAL	Lazuli

Guideline Divinatory Meanings:

Keywords (Upright): Good fortune, eternity, new cycles, change

Upright – Effortless success. Good fortune that is unexpected. Coincidences. Luck. The beginning of a new cycle. Advancement. Positive upheaval. Change. A card of good fortune, the appearance of destiny and Karmic change.

The Wheel of Fortune is a card of fantastic, great positive change. In many respects, this card is one that suggests you have got a good chance of getting the finances you require or the job you wanted, or you will succeed at what you set out to do. Obviously, nothing is ever guaranteed, but with The Wheel of Fortune in your spread, you certainly have a positive omen on your side. This is a card of good luck, fortune, and change, and this is change for the better. However, in order to fully succeed, you must also be prepared to adapt to this change and be open to it and work with it. This is a card of good luck.

- When the wheel spins around, luck and fortune can be found.

Keywords (Reversed): Guard against a discordant environment, recognize good from evil, curb gambling, dark before the dawn, delays

Ill Dignified or Reversed – Unexpected circumstances. Resistance to change. Unexpected interruptions. A warning against gambling. Difficulties. Delays.

The Wheel of Fortune reversed can be interpreted in a number of ways, particularly because it is just that, a wheel and one that moves around in a cycle. Taken simply, if The Wheel of Fortune is all about good fortune then reversed it may be possible to say that The Wheel of Fortune is all about bad luck. However, this is far too simplistic. For example, was the Wheel in motion before it settled on the reversed position? If this is the case, then maybe the card reversed is purely the end of a cycle of good luck and nothing whatsoever to do with bad luck. Or is it that the card reversed is stuck in the upside down position? If this is the case, then maybe there is room for movement back up, but until the Wheel is no longer stationary and gets going again, then pathways and energies are blocked. There is also a question about which way the Wheel is turning and what is encountered along the way. Something that should be positive like a promotion for example, may become burdensome over time, so something lucky changes to something unlucky. Either way, whether this card is upright or reversed, it is about luck and fortune. It does not matter if it is a turn for the worse at the moment because the Wheel will keep on turning and finally end any periods of difficulty.

- When luck and fortune are running low, spin the wheel, and off you go.

XI Justice

Justice (La Justice)
The Daughter of the Lords of Truth
The Ruler of the Balance

CARD NUMBER	11
KEY NUMBER	22
RULERSHIP	Libra
HEBREW LETTER	Lamed
TRANSLATION	Ox Goad (Noun) to Teach or Instruct (Verb)
NUMERICAL VALUE	12
ASTROLOGICAL ASSOCIATIONS	Neptune
CANDLE	Gray
CRYSTAL	Jade

Guideline Divinatory Meanings:

Keywords (Upright): Decisions, resolution of strife, honesty, reap what you sow

Upright – Amicable and favorable resolution of conflicts. Triumph over bigotry and prejudice. Legal action. Litigation. Contracts. Settlement. Divorce. Sometimes marriage, depending upon the other cards and normally only when marriage contracts, legal or financial documents are a necessary part of the intended union. Clarity. Fairness. Arbitration. A straightforward choice. Judgement.

The Justice card is symbolic of the resolution of conflicts. If there are issues in your life at the moment that may need attention, then it is possible that you will have some hard unwelcome choices to make, possibly contractual or legal in nature. However hard these choices are though, it is most certainly with a positive end in mind. The card is often symbolic of partnership or marriage issues, particularly in a legal sense. Depending upon other cards, marriage is sometimes foretold and also legalities relating to marriage. If you have a partner, honesty is most certainly the best policy here. It is important to take a firm and balanced view in everything that you do, as you will reap what you sow, but don't worry, because good counsel will be at hand.

- In the game of life, reap what you sow; if you have been good, then you'll soon know.
- A card of legal issues.

Keywords (Reversed): Injustice, inequality, hidden forces at work, overcome any ill will with good, fear defeats purpose

Ill Dignified or Reversed – Injustice. Inequality and bias. Separations not yet ratified or legalized. Delay. Imbalance. Confusion surrounding legal or tax affairs. Complicated negotiations. Unfair or delayed judgement.

The Justice card reversed is clear, where fairness, balance and honesty are all part of the Justice card, when it is reversed all of the opposites apply. This reversed card is all about unfairness, imbalance, and dishonesty. To take it to its extreme, if this card was turned on its head, then the tools of justice, such as the scales, are not only blocked from working, but they disappear entirely as they crash to the floor. This can be symbolic of a total breakdown of the legal system, such as corrupt judges and witnesses and dubious evidence. When this card appears reversed in a spread, then it is possible that you are in a situation or dealing with a situation that you feel is clearly unfair. It is a card about feeling somewhat badly done to. Whatever it is that you need, you may feel that you are not getting enough of it, whatever it is. In a relationship reading, this card implies that any legal situations may drag on. Justice will be served with this card reversed in a spread. However, it may not necessarily be what is perceived as being fair, so the best advice is to ensure to plan for all eventualities.

- When the verdict's not right, and much said untrue, try to move on, it's the best thing to do.

XII The Hanged Man

The Hanged Man (Le Pendu)
The Spirit of the Mighty Waters

CARD NUMBER	12
KEY NUMBER	23
RULERSHIP	Water
HEBREW LETTER	Mem
TRANSLATION	Water
NUMERICAL VALUE	3
ASTROLOGICAL ASSOCIATIONS	Pisces
CANDLE	Dark Green
CRYSTAL	Blue Lace Agate

Guideline Divinatory Meanings:

Keywords (Upright): Surrender to circumstance, suspension, rebirth, transition, sacrifices in the present to reap benefits in the future

Upright – Devotion to a worthwhile cause. Temporary suspension of progress. Flexibility of mind and a willingness to adapt to changes. Sacrifice in the present to reap benefit in the future. A waiting period. Rebirth. Sacrificing one thing to obtain another. Transformation. Circumstances literally turned on their head.

The Hanged Man, at first, may appear a card of discomfort or even death as we observe a man suspended upside down. Indeed, the man hanging upside down in the card is very much alive and he is in a contemplative mood. He is actually looking for enlightenment, and as he does, he is suspended in time as he follows his quest for knowledge and spiritual knowledge. When The Hanged Man card turns up in a spread, it symbolizes a need to take calculated inaction to solve any problems or challenges facing you at the moment. This card warns that now is not the time to swim against the tide, but with it, even though being pushed down stream may take you temporarily away from your destination. Do not worry, you will arrive at the place where you want to be. You just need to make tiny adjustments that will set you free from this temporary period of unrest and set you back on the right path so that you can move forward with confidence.

- When feeling down and in a state, it's time to relax and meditate.

Keywords (Reversed): Better the devil you know, wasted effort, try to forgive your enemies, material world may dominate the soul

Ill Dignified or Reversed – Lack of growth. Lack of commitment. Preoccupation with selfish and material things. Despite drawbacks a preference for the status quo. Stagnation. Apathy in pursuit of goals. Taking the view "Better the devil you know." Failure to act with an inability to move forward or progress.

The Hanged Man reversed is quite an ironic image because when he is in the reversed position, he is actually in his upright position, but he won't get far with a rope still shackled around his leg. In its upright position, this is a card of self sacrifice in order to achieve greater things for himself or others. When he is reversed there is no sacrifice, he is now on terra firma, with no periods of suspension or reflection; therefore, he is free to take up more selfish and materialistic pursuits. When The Hanged Man reversed shows up in your spread, then it could be a time to become less materialistic. To achieve what you require, you may have to accept that there will be no gain unless there is some pain and trying to avoid this is pointless. Try not to resist a re-ordering of priorities and maybe a new sense of purpose is required. Try to fulfill not only materialistic wants and desires but look to more spiritual ones as well.

- To succeed may take some pain, but always trust there will be gain. Let spiritual enlightenment be your aim.

XIII Death

Death (La Mort)
The Child of the Great Transformers
The Lord of the Gate of Death

CARD NUMBER	13
KEY NUMBER	24
RULERSHIP	Scorpio
HEBREW LETTER	Nun
TRANSLATION	Fish
NUMERICAL VALUE	12
ASTROLOGICAL ASSOCIATIONS	Aries
CANDLE	Dark Brown
CRYSTAL	Malachite

Guideline Divinatory Meanings:

Keywords (Upright): Sweeping changes, expect the unexpected, embrace the unknown

Upright – The beginning of a new life as a result of underlying circumstances. Transformation, and change. Major changes. The end of a phase in life which has served its purpose. Abrupt and complete change of circumstances, way of life, and patterns of behavior due to past events and actions. Alterations.

The Death card is often one of the most feared cards in a Tarot reading, but this has more to do with what is shown in the movies as opposed to the true meaning of the card. In fact, the Death card very rarely means the death of anyone. The Death card signifies change and the end of a cycle, the end of a situation, or even the end to a series of events. You need to let go of the past and accept that things are going to change in a major way. If you are in a relationship, it may mean that the relationship is nearing the end of its natural cycle and has run its course, but it can also signify deep change in that relationship. If you are feeling somewhat low at the moment, then do not despair because this card can be likened to the phoenix rising from the ashes. Although change is sometimes difficult to come to terms with; you will emerge from the whole situation a much stronger and wiser person. Remember that death is not the end; it is simply what comes before resurrection or rebirth. When this card appears, the advice is to go with the flow, accept any change, and move on from the past with a new attitude and renewed positivity.

- The trick is to accept that the past is gone, onwards and upwards, it's time to move on.

Keywords (Reversed): Rise above materialism, guard against impulsiveness, fear of change

Ill Dignified or Reversed – Change that may not necessarily be welcomed. A refusal to face the fear of change or change itself. Difficult periods of transition. Inertia. Lethargy. Mental, physical or emotional exhaustion.

The Death card reversed, unlike its upright counterpart that is all about endings, is all about things not coming to an end. On the face of it, this might seem like a positive thing; however, imagine being at a party that drags on and on. Instead of all the revellers, leaving on a high, they roll out worse for wear onto the street, having overstayed their welcome. Some of them may even be feeling quite exhausted and sick. Another example might be a neverending feast where too much of a good thing on tap leads to obesity or health issues related to becoming fat from the spoils. Either way, this lack of an ending maybe isn't such a positive thing. In order for things to change, and more importantly for things to be reborn, then there has to be an ending, regardless of how good the present situation may be. When Death is turned upside down, he falls off his horse, his bones crash to the floor, and his horse lands upside down. He can also no longer wield his scythe and he has almost become a figure of ridicule or a mockery of death itself. Therefore, when this card appears upside down in a spread, it may be time to let go. You may need to recognize when something has come to its natural end. Try not to resist change as this could lead to stagnation in the present situation. It is important to recognize when to let go and move on. You may need to accept that all good things need to come to an end if better things are to happen.

- Some things are better when put to bed. Accept that the past should really lie dead. There's a million problems Karma will bring, when you have too much of a good thing.

XIV Temperance

Temperance (Temperance)
The Daughter of the Reconcilers
The Bringer Forth of Life

CARD NUMBER	14
KEY NUMBER	25
RULERSHIP	Sagittarius
HEBREW LETTER	Samech
TRANSLATION	Prop
NUMERICAL VALUE	12
ASTROLOGICAL ASSOCIATIONS	Taurus
CANDLE	Lilac
CRYSTAL	Turquoise

Guideline Divinatory Meanings:

Keywords (Upright): Caution, diplomacy, risk, diligence to reach your goals, keep company with harmonious people

Upright – Combination. Cooperation. Coordination. Innovation through combination. Diplomacy. Successful negotiations. Maturity in dealing with certain matters. A placid, balanced temperament and good outlook. Meaning literally, temperance in the sense of harmony and balance. Good management. An ability to adapt to changing circumstances.

The Temperance card on the face of it is one of moderation, keeping portion sizes small and a "little bit of what you fancy does you good" and keep a lid on your temper. However, the Temperance card goes much deeper than this and it is often symbolic of bringing opposing elements or factions together and by skillfully combining them, a positive end result can be achieved. This is a card of skillfully combining spiritual wisdom with the impulsiveness of temperament. It is a card about achieving balance which will be obtained by a careful blend of both patience and self control. If you are already in a relationship, this card may mean that developments in that relationship are about to take place. Choose your tools wisely particularly if you are trying to resolve family matters or bring together opposing factions. Just like a pen and a piece of paper, on their own they are simply objects, but use them together to write and you can produce something else better than the individual objects themselves. Moderation in all areas of your life is brought by Temperance, but also the ability to bring joy, harmony and balance to any stressful situation.

- Correct ingredients thrown into the mix, will help with any problems to fix.

Keywords (Reversed): Imbalance, poor judgement, fickle decisions, passionless love, possessiveness repels your heart's desire

Ill Dignified or Reversed – Imbalance. Volatility. Poor judgement. Fickle decisions. Conflicting interests. Physical stress. Disagreements. Restlessness and instability. Trying to combine too many or the wrong elements in too short an expanse of time.

The Temperance card reversed is all about the combination of elements that may not necessarily be the right mix. Whereas Temperance in the upright position signifies the skillful combination of elements to achieve positive ends; the mixture produced by the Temperance card reversed is not so sweet. Imagine trying to mix oil and water, the formula just doesn't work as one ingredient repels the other. This idea can also be likened to people, families, and nations. If the mix is not right, then acrimonious situations can arise. Therefore, when Temperance reversed turns up in a spread, it is time to assess how to deal with certain situations. Perhaps some things are better kept separate than brought together. The reversed Temperance card can also be symbolic of conflicts which may be external (involving other people) or internal between your higher and lower self. Try to guard against selfishness, as this could lead to divisions in a number of scenarios. For those in business now, it is a good time to steer clear of conflicts and now may not be the best time for forming relationships.

- Oil and water do not mix. Not unless you've got a box of tricks.

XV The Devil

The Devil (Le Diable)
The Lord of the Gates of Matter
The Child of the Forces of Time

CARD NUMBER	15
KEY NUMBER	26
RULERSHIP	Capricorn
HEBREW LETTER	Ayin
TRANSLATION	Eye
NUMERICAL VALUE	12
ASTROLOGICAL ASSOCIATIONS	Saturn
CANDLE	Ochre
CRYSTAL	Obsidian

Guideline Divinatory Meanings:

Keywords (Upright): Magic, self enforced restrictions, addictions, mystery, wants and desires, cruelty hurts only the giver

Upright – Money matters. Feeling the burden of the material side of life. Desire for physical and material things. Feelings of frustration and oppression. A tendency to collect and hoard money and material objects. Lust. Obsession and self imposed constraints. The querent's knowledge of his or her own needs, wants, and desires. Security versus creative or spiritual fulfilment.

The Devil card, just like the Death card is one of the most misunderstood cards in a Tarot deck. If you look closely at the Devil in a traditional pack, you will see that this card is not really the Devil at all. In fact, he is a creature that is half god and half goat; he is Pan the half-goat god of nature and/or Dionysius. The godly side of him brings out your deepest desires and passions, whereas the beast in him helps to enslave you by them. This card tends to suggest that you are placing restrictions upon yourself, but either you don't realize it, or you believe that there is nothing that can be done about it. You are being driven by your baser instincts and you may even feel that you cannot escape the situation you find yourself in. However, this is not the case. Your free will is not lost and you need to take responsibility for yourself and your actions. In business you may find that you have a strong preoccupation with money and material things and a reluctance to change in this area could be at the expense of growth. Free yourself from any temptations or addictions that you may have; you really can do it.

- Find the strength to break your chains, you'll be rewarded for all your pains.

Keywords (Reversed): Undermining influences at work, greed brings eventual unhappiness, replace coldness with warmth

Ill Dignified or Reversed – Abuse of authority. Material success is the focus to the exclusion of all other things. Uncontrolled ambition. Greed. Ties to a person or situation or thing. Emotional blackmail. More severe forms of the above. Darkness.

The Devil card reversed in its simplest interpretation, is that, those who were once bound by his chains are now free, because his hold over them comes crashing down in the same way he does when he falls upside down. However, there are deeper meanings to the Devil card reversed. When he appears in a spread he can also signify a person or persons who are denying themselves even the slightest of pleasures for fear of addiction. If you think about the Devil upright as being a card of sex, drugs, and rock and roll, this is a card of the alcoholic who daren't even have the slightest drink for fear of becoming enslaved by it. So whereas, yes, this card reversed can indicate a breaking free of one's obsessions, it is important to ensure that new obsessions aren't being created to replace them. When this card appears, now might be a good time to get rid of any psychological chains. It is important to listen to your heart as well as your head because a purely intellectual approach could be somewhat tedious and boring for you right now. If you heart desires liberation, then it may be a good time to give into it. Should you be feeling somewhat power hungry at this time, then try to curb this. In a relationship, this card can indicate that one of the partners may be feeling a little tied down. A good way to think about this card is that when the Devil is on his head on the floor, now might be the appropriate time to break the chains and set yourself free.

- Remember in life there is always a choice, listen to your heart and your inner voice.

Hidden Meaning: The Devil card in a spiritual position may indicate someone who is out of control and that something may need to be done about it. The Nine of Wands reversed, together with the Devil, may indicate that someone has a potential drinking problem.

XVI The Tower

The Tower (La Maison Dieu)
The Lord of the Hosts of the Mighty

CARD NUMBER	16
KEY NUMBER	27
RULERSHIP	Mars
HEBREW LETTER	Peh
TRANSLATION	Mouth
NUMERICAL VALUE	9
ASTROLOGICAL ASSOCIATIONS	Mars
CANDLE	Vanilla
CRYSTAL	Red Agate

Guideline Divinatory Meanings:

Keywords (Upright): Change that cannot be avoided, reap what is sown, the paralysis of evil by love

Upright – Disruption. Conflict. Change. Sudden revelations. Overthrow of an existing way of life. Major occurrences. Disturbance of well-worn routines. Dramatic upheaval. Change of residence or job, sometimes both. Widespread repercussions of actions. In the end, enlightenment and freedom.

The Tower card, as with the Death and Devil cards, tend to cause the greatest amount of concern. However, unlike the latter two, The Tower card really is one that offers a warning. The Tower card shows a tower that is built on false beliefs and lies. A thunderbolt of lightning strikes from above to shatter those beliefs and preconceptions. Although you may not realize it now, things are going to change. This card warns of a very rude awakening, because everything may not be what it seems. The Tower suggests the collapsing of the norm in favor of something much deeper and better. This card is indicative that change is coming. However, no matter how disturbing any revelations that may come to light, or alterations to your life, please be assured that you will see that in the end it is all for the best. When this card shows up in your spread, the most effective way to tackle it, is to accept that old outdated forms will come tumbling down, but this will inevitably give rise to bigger and better things in your life. Freedom and enlightenment are starred.

- All the lies are laid out and bare, move quickly on, don't stop and stare.

Keywords (Reversed): Negativity, restricted desires, develop the self to avert risk

Ill Dignified or Reversed – Less severe forms of the above. Negativity. Restriction of desires and feelings of confinement. Drastic change that may affect freedom of expression. Sometimes financial issues and imprisonment. More usually imprisonment within a set of circumstances which cannot currently be altered. Sudden changes out of one's control.

The Tower card reversed is an odd card to deal with because when The Tower is turned on its head, instead of it being an unstable structure, it actually becomes quite firm in its foundations. If The Tower in the upright position is one that is built on falsehoods and lies, then The Tower reversed, without any lightning to strike it down, suggests that those lies and falsehoods are to remain on a firm footing. When The Tower is in the upright position any liars come crashing out of the windows when it is hit by lightning. (This is the usual portrayal of The Tower). However, when The Tower is upside down, they can simply crawl back in and continue to perpetuate their lies. For this reason, anything that should have been revealed is destined to remain hidden. Sometimes it is better to have a sudden revelation of truth no matter how painful at the time, than to maintain a status quo that is built on a foundation of lies. In the upright position The Tower informs the querent no matter how painful the truth is. However, in its reversed position The Tower allows the querent not to hear what should be heard. Sometimes the truth hurts, but sometimes it is even worse if it is kept secret for any length of time. At its worst, The Tower reversed could be symbolic of a cover up or scam. As the querent tries to uncover the truth, the liars are not illuminated by the thunder bolt of lightning and continue to remain hidden. The advice here is clear: When this card shows up, there is a need to look deeper into any given set of circumstances. All may not be what it seems. Therefore, as is stated in the keywords, try to develop the self to avert risk. Don't allow yourself to become imprisoned within circumstances that you cannot alter; and if something looks too good to be true, then there is a possibility that it probably is.

- Things below are not what they are on top. Proceed with caution to avoid a sharp drop.

XVII The Star

The Star (L'Etoile)
The Daughter of the Firmament
The Dweller Between the Waters

CARD NUMBER	17
KEY NUMBER	28
RULERSHIP	Aquarius
HEBREW LETTER	Tzaddi
TRANSLATION	Fish Hook
NUMERICAL VALUE	12
ASTROLOGICAL ASSOCIATIONS	Gemini
CANDLE	Pale Yellow
CRYSTAL	Amber

Guideline Divinatory Meanings:

Keywords (Upright): Faith, look positively to the future; truth, hope, or faith, do not limit yourself, distinguish reality from illusion

Upright – Fresh hope and renewal. Healing of old wounds. Hope. Renewal of faith and hope. Spiritual love. A mental and physical broadening of horizons. Promise and fulfilment. Inspiration. Influence over others. Vigor and confidence. Protection.

The Star is often one of the most beautifully depicted cards in a Tarot deck and its meaning is very positive, too. The Star is a card of the future. Although, unlike many other cards, it does not indicate massive change in your life, but it does mean that any negativity is being left behind. This means that if there is any change, it will be very positive in nature. With The Star card in your spread, you are likely to feel a sense of relief and inner calm, indeed you may even feel a sense of liberation, as if a weight has been lifted from your shoulders. You may even be thinking about embarking upon a course of study, but right now the possibilities in your life are endless. Clarity of vision, spiritual insight, healing energy, hope, and help all accompany this card. Within a relationship, this card is all about giving each other space and freedom to help make things work.

- Love and light all problems gone. With a happy heart it's time to move on.
- A "Wish" card.

Keywords (Reversed): Stubbornness, an inability to adapt, lack of trust, truth demands a blending of heart and mind

Ill Dignified or Reversed – Self doubt. Stubbornness. Unwillingness or inability to adapt to changing circumstances and accept the opportunities it may bring. Lack of trust and self-distrust. Obstacles to happiness. Inability to freely express oneself. Rigidity of mind.

The Star reversed, unlike its upright self, is not about a guiding light into the future; it is more about a period of darkness. If you imagine The Star upside down, it would fall into the waters below and have its warm illuminating glow extinguished. It is a gloomy picture, and at its worst, The Star is the height of pessimism, an all-pervading darkness. It is a feeling that things are just going to get worse. There is a sense with this card reversed that it is all bad, a complete and polar opposite from its other self upright. However, nothing is ever that clear cut. There is also a sense that The Star could just be hidden behind the clouds waiting to suddenly appear again. For this reason, it is always important to trust that things happen for a reason and there will be light at the end of the tunnel. At the very least, night follows day and day follows night and the darkness is never around forever. The clouds will part and The Star will shine again; it's just a case of finding the best way to navigate your way round the obstacles in the gloom.

- Try to nurture that initial spark, as it will help guide you, through the dark.

XVIII The Moon

The Moon (La Lune)
The Ruler of the Flux & Reflux
The Child of the Sons of the Mighty

CARD NUMBER	18
KEY NUMBER	29
RULERSHIP	Pisces
HEBREW LETTER	Qoph
TRANSLATION	The Back of the Head
NUMERICAL VALUE	12
ASTROLOGICAL ASSOCIATIONS	Cancer
CANDLE	Jasmine
CRYSTAL	Aquamarine

Guideline Divinatory Meanings:

Keywords (Upright): Intuition, the subconscious mind, dreams, innate wisdom

Upright – Imagination. Dreams and psychic impressions. Sometimes psychic work. Illusions. Inability to see things clearly sometimes resulting in a low mood. Sometimes signifies fiction writing or acting, particularly work in the entertainment industry. Difficulty organizing daily life. The unconscious mind.

The Moon is a card that represents two alternatives. You can either be sucked into the stream of uncertainty, strangeness, and weirdness that may presently appear to be in your surroundings; or you can hop onto your boat and float your way through it – all using the strength and wisdom of your inner being. This card is symbolic of needing to listen to your inner voice and take notice of it. When The Moon card appears in your spread, it brings with it a caution that you should not take things at face value because much deeper things may be hidden from your view. You will be able to find all of the answers that you require, as long as you pay attention to that little inner voice in your head, namely your intuition. For those already in a relationship, then this card brings with it a sense of urgency to resolve any conflicts or issues. When this card appears, always listen to your subconscious. Now could be a particularly creative period for you and you need to harness that creative energy to a positive end. Try to steer clear of indulging too heavily in things like smoking and alcohol, etc., as this will only inhibit you in your decision making. Listen to your intuitive dreams as they are trying to guide you.

- Look for those deeper things hidden from view, this is important, something essential to do.
- A card of caution and a card of women and for women and female issues. Also an "Illusion" card.

Keywords (Reversed): Need for secrecy, illusion, escape into fantasy to avoid reality, look beneath the glamour of appearance

Ill Dignified or Reversed – Exaggerated forms of the above. The need for secrecy. Deception. Illusion. Escape into daydreams to avoid dealing with reality. Inability to discern fact from fiction. Insincere people. Hidden forces. Trickery. Sometimes problems with telling the truth. False friends. Silence is golden.

The Moon card reversed, in some respects, is like The Star reversed. When these cards are turned upside down, their lights become extinguished; however, when The Moon card falls into the water, the creatures of the night land on top. It's almost as if a fallen dark moon has in a figurative sense given a safe haven to creatures with baser instincts. For example, criminals who lurk in the dark – stalkers, burglars, muggers etc. – would be very happy to bask in the darkness afforded by The Moon reversed. At its best, The Moon upright is a card about strangeness and weirdness and a stream of uncertainty. It is bad enough having to cope with a dreamy landscape in daylight, let alone in a dark, moonless environment. At its very worst, the moon reversed can be symbolic of social discord and breakdown. On an individual level, it can signify dark periods of depression or mental health issues. Neither this card upright or reversed is particularly welcome in a spread, so it is important to choose your friends carefully. Keep your friends close, but keep your enemies closer still. Keep your own counsel, as now might not be a good time for revealing any of your inner secrets. But always remember just as with The Star reversed, night follows day, as day follows night, so ride out any periods of uncertainty or bewilderment and wait for the breaking dawn.

- All that glitters is not gold; how often, have you so been told?

Hidden Meaning: The Moon, together with the High Priestess, may signify gynecological issues and also psychic ability. The Moon with the Seven of Swords warns about who to trust and to be careful with money. The Moon with the Three of Swords warns against ill health.

XIX The Sun

The Sun (Le Soleil)
The Lord of the Fire of the World

CARD NUMBER	19
KEY NUMBER	30
RULERSHIP	The Sun
HEBREW LETTER	Resh
TRANSLATION	The Head
NUMERICAL VALUE	9
ASTROLOGICAL ASSOCIATIONS	Leo
CANDLE	Gold
CRYSTAL	Clear Quartz

Guideline Divinatory Meanings:

Keywords (Upright): Health, vitality, creative energy, and, above all, success

Upright – Contentment and happiness on attaining success. Good health. Material happiness. Mental, physical, and spiritual vitality. New inventors or inventions. Academic and particularly scientific success. Reward. Acclaim. Approval. Children. Abundance of energy. Achievement. Joy and happiness.

The Sun is possibly one of the nicest cards to have in a spread. If you have been having a hard time recently, then this card signifies the end of the dark days and the start of the sunshine. This card is an incredibly positive card that brings with it feelings of inner peace, contentment, and hope. The Sun signifies good health and it brings energy and vitality with it. Promotion and career prospects are well starred and so too the attainment of your desired goals. You may also find that your creativity is at a high point and that you could reach for the stars. This card has also been associated with the conception and/or birth of a much-wanted baby and relationships may grow deeper, especially if effort is put into them. An altogether wonderful card; lucky you!

- With joy and love and happiness, fear not your question; the answer is yes.
- This is a "Yes" card.

Keywords (Reversed): Marriage and relationship issues, maintain the sanctity of marriage, align spiritual, physical, and mental goals

Ill Dignified or Reversed – Troubled partnerships and marriages. Diminished forms of the above. Broken engagements and contracts. Sometimes, educational issues or allergies. Hyperactivity. Arrogance. Relationship issues. Vanity. Hypersensitivity. Misjudgement. Delayed happiness.

The Sun card reversed is very similar in nature to The Moon and The Star reversed. In its upright position The Star is a very optimistic card. It is one of the nicest cards in the pack to have in a spread and success and happiness is starred. But imagine The Sun reversed. As it turns upside down, it's blindingly happy light begins to fade as it sinks below the horizon. But unlike The Moon and The Star, to lose The Sun wouldn't simply mean just a loss of light; it would mean a world that was left in complete chaos, bereft of all of its life-giving benefits. Of course, this is an extreme scenario. It may just be a case that the clouds are blocking the Sun's rays, which would mean a period lacking clarity. It might also mean a period of feeling jaded and a time of discord. But just as with The Moon and Star reversed, night follows day and day once again follows night. For this reason, The Sun card reversed offers you success, but only when you have overcome any obstacles in your way. In some circumstances, The Sun reversed may indicate issues surrounding a pregnancy or birth. In a relationship, it is possible that one of the partners may be too competitive and this can be true when relating to business as well. You need to trust that happiness, although it may have been delayed, will eventually be yours.

- Fearing the question off you go, but there's always hope; it's not a no.

XX Judgement

Judgement (Le Jugement)
The Spirit of the Primal Fire

CARD NUMBER	20
KEY NUMBER	31
RULERSHIP	Fire
HEBREW LETTER	Shin
TRANSLATION	Tooth
NUMERICAL VALUE	3
ASTROLOGICAL ASSOCIATIONS	Moon
CANDLE	Indigo
CRYSTAL	Amethyst

Guideline Divinatory Meanings:

Keywords (Upright): Clear thinking, spiritual growth, awakening, resurrection

Upright – Changes and improvements. Satisfactory outcome to a specific matter or period of life. Joy in accomplishment. Awakening. Rebirth. A good time for career moves. Renewed health, vitality, and mental clarity. Sometimes indicates important pending decisions that will change the pattern of life for the better.

The Judgement card often shows the dead rising from their graves and an angel blowing a trumpet over them. This imagery is symbolic of things that were dead and almost buried, but never fully resolved. These issues may now be moving to the forefront of your consciousness. Everything has come out into the open just like the dead from their graves, and in order to move forward, you need to put everything back into the past where it belongs. If you have had any health issues lately, then this is a good card for you, as it signifies healing and a period of recovery. This card is also synonymous with change. You may find that you have some big decisions coming up that will involve firmly shutting the door on the past and taking a leap of faith into the future. This card is certainly one of leaving the past behind and closing the door, but it is also one of decision making and change. If you are single or hoping for a new relationship, then this is also a good card to have in your spread. Indeed, on many levels, all that is required is for you to remain true to yourself and go after what you want.

- Put the past back in its chest, so you can move on and be your best.
- A "Rebirth" card.

Keywords (Reversed): Stagnation, delay in finishing a series of actions, a fear of death and change, rise above any emotional turmoil

Ill Dignified or Reversed – Stagnation. Delay in concluding a series of actions. Fear of change and sometimes fear of death. Lack of progress due to lack of important decision making. Separations that are not necessarily permanent. Guilt. A broader outlook. Turning a page in life. Where one door closes another one opens.

The Judgment card reversed is not about things that are dead and buried but not quite resolved, nor is it about awakening or rebirth; this is a card that shouts about the past coming back to haunt. Imagine this card turned upside down. People are falling out of their coffins. Figuratively speaking, this is a reversed card of the undead that hang about and make a complete nuisance of themselves. Instead of a rebirth or an awakening in a positive sense, this is a card indicative more of a vampire fest set to sap your lifeblood. This could mean that you are not able to continue your spiritual growth. With all of those vampires around, you might even feel that you have a fear of death itself. In a situation like this, the best way forward is to make sure that the demons are placed firmly back in their coffins with a metaphorical stake through their hearts, if that is what it takes. Let the past become dead and buried and let it stay that way. Seize the day and make things happen or face the guilt and regret that you maybe could have done better. Remember, sometimes it's really good to slam the door firmly on the past so that a new one can open in the future.

- Slam the door on the past, so you can, finally, be free at last.

XXI The World

The World (Le Monde)
The Great One of the Night of Time

CARD NUMBER	21
KEY NUMBER	32
RULERSHIP	Saturn
HEBREW LETTER	Tau
TRANSLATION	Cross
NUMERICAL VALUE	9
ASTROLOGICAL ASSOCIATIONS	Sun
CANDLE	Multicolored
CRYSTAL	Onyx

Guideline Divinatory Meanings:

Keywords (Upright): Moving onwards and upwards, achievement, attainment, success

Upright – Accomplishment. Fulfilment. Completion of a personal cycle, project, series of events or chapter in life. Success. A culmination of events. A sense of repleteness.

The World is a card of accomplishment and the end of an event or series of events. It is a period where something that has been striven for finally comes to fruition. For example, a writer getting their novel published or an Olympian winning his/her first gold medal or even someone completing their final thesis that leads to their doctorate (PhD). The World also symbolizes travel, not necessarily short journeys, but deep, rewarding journeys. You may also find that if you have embarked upon a large project or period of study that was successful, then your talents will become highly sought after. This is a card of lasting success and no matter what you do or where you go, you will certainly feel comfortable in your own skin.

- Success is yours, achieved at last; enjoy the attainments from your past.

Keywords (Reversed): Frustration, distrust, fear of change, application of willpower

Ill Dignified or Reversed – Frustration. Completion delayed. Sometimes fear of change. Inability to bring something to a satisfactory end. Resistance to change. Lack of trust. Despite appearances to the contrary, an indication that events have not yet come to a conclusion but are nearing completion. Hesitation.

The World card reversed can be symbolic of stagnation and failure to complete something. As an opposite to The World card in its upright position, lack of travel is starred, as opposed to deep rewarding journeys. In the extreme, this reversed card can even be one of agoraphobia and a fear of stepping outdoors, let alone traveling anywhere. It can also be symbolic of someone who thinks that they are worldly wise, but, in fact, they are probably very naïve. It can also tell of someone who is fooling themselves into thinking that they know more than they do. Sometimes projects that appear complete can often be frustratingly near to completion, but just not quite there yet. When The World card reversed turns up in a spread, the best advice is not to hesitate; put your best foot forward and build up the momentum to complete anything that you have started. Don't resist change and don't make out that you know more than you do. Remember, just because the time may not be quite right at the moment to make any changes, finish projects or make those necessary journeys. The time to do all of this will come round again because your roundabout of a world does keep on turning and it's not time to get off yet.

- Move swiftly forward and forge ahead, change is something, you should not dread.

Ace Wands
The Root of the Powers of Fire

NUMERICAL VALUE	5
SEASON	Spring
DIRECTION	South
ELEMENT	Fire
TETRAGRAMMATRON	Yod (Primal Energy)
LIFE ASPECT	Career and Enterprise
ASTROLOGICAL ASSOCIATIONS	Leo, Aries, Sagittarius

Guideline Divinatory Meanings:

Keywords (Upright): New beginnings, good results, business trips, a new venture, a phone call

Upright – An exciting new project or career. The essence of fire, creativity, inventiveness, ambition, and enthusiasm. The aggressive pursuit of new ventures. Foundations for future success, intuition, conception, fertility, artistic innovation, and manhood.

The Ace of Wands is symbolic of launching oneself with great enthusiasm into an exciting new project or career. This card in your spread would suggest that you are now ready to put any new plans into action with all of the creative energy that you need. This is the start of your journey and you may find that you have feelings of spiritual awakening and enlightenment. This card can also suggest travel and/or the start of a new relationship. With the Ace of Wands in your spread, you should be feeling ready to conquer the world!

- Off to fields and pastures new. Go and show what you can do.

Keywords (Reversed): Demanding challenges, avarice, greed, over confidence

Ill Dignified or Reversed – Starkness, impotence, unfruitfulness, avarice, greed. Unproductive over confidence. In a woman's spread, this card may indicate trouble with men.

The Ace of Wands reversed, unlike its upright counterpart, is not about new beginnings. The upright card is *very much* about new beginnings and if you think of Aces generally as the spark that ignites the fire, then the Ace of Wands reversed lacks this initial energy. The Ace of Wands normally points upwards to the sky, but imagine if it was turned on its head; it would become rooted to the spot and unable to move in any direction. This could signify that you could be finding it difficult to start things at the moment, or maybe anything you have started is getting delayed. You may even feel that there is something that you should be excited about, but you just can't seem to muster the enthusiasm for it. There is a warning to guard against being overconfident in any new situations and to avoid being generally greedy. In a relationship, you may find that the results that you are hoping for do not materialize. However, this card is not all about doom and gloom because when the Ace of Wands reversed is rooted to the spot, it is like the static stone that actually gathers moss. Therefore, during any periods of creative blocks, take the opportunity to recharge your batteries and collect up your creative energy to be ready to start again soon.

- If at first you don't succeed, keep the faith; it's all you need.

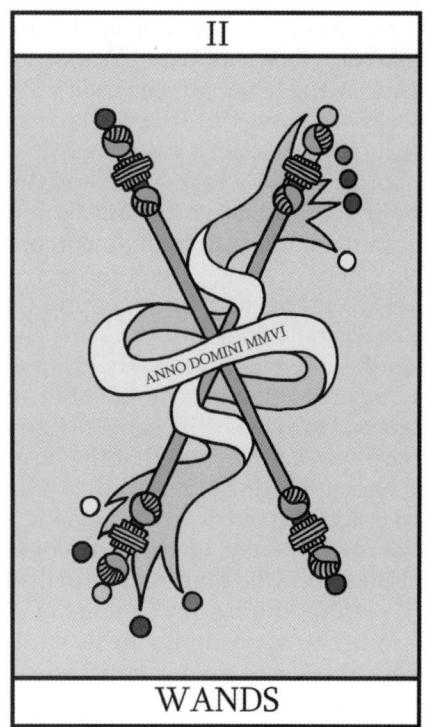

II Wands
The Lord of Dominion

NUMERICAL VALUE	2
ELEMENT	Fire
TETRAGRAMMATRON	Yod (Primal Energy)
LIFE ASPECT	Career and Enterprise
ASTROLOGICAL ASSOCIATIONS	Leo, Aries, Sagittarius

Guideline Divinatory Meanings:

Keywords (Upright): Choices, making the right choice, channelling energy in the right direction, obstacles resolved through analysis

Upright – Success that has been achieved through hard work. Strength of character and will, ensuring that ideas come to fruition. The responsible use of power and wisdom gained through experience. Wealth obtained legally. Job-related perks.

The Two of Wands is a card of choice, where you may find yourself faced with two options and it will be up to you to use your inner wisdom and judgment to make the right choice. Depending upon which literature is studied, this card is also symbolic of new projects and new goals in life, but you must carefully weigh up the alternatives. Opportunities are starred relating to partnerships and this may involve some travel or moving away. You may also find that you have reached a crossroads with a relationship and this could be either choosing to end a relationship, start a new relationship, or move the existing relationship to a deeper level of commitment. This card is one that definitely brings with it a set of choices.

- When success is based on choice, always listen to that inner voice.

Keywords (Reversed): Naked ambition that knows no bounds, fortune obtained through unorthodox means

Ill Dignified or Reversed – Naked ambition that knows no bounds. Attainment of a worthless ambition. Riches and fortune obtained by questionable means. Sometimes loss of faith in one's own rationale and oneself.

The Two of Wands reversed just like its upright counterpart is about choice and balance. However because the Wands in their reversed position become off balance, tip over and lie on the floor it becomes difficult to choose the better one because they are not in their normal positions. In business and relationships previous balance and harmony may be giving way to discord and some arguments may arise. This card reversed in a spread also suggests that you might be questioning your achievements. For example was what you did actually worthwhile? The best way to negotiate this card in a spread is to weigh up any choices carefully, steer clear of any dubious means of obtaining wealth and try to maintain an even handed approach to any persons or situations around you.

- Can't decide which way to turn, it's simply a case of live and learn.

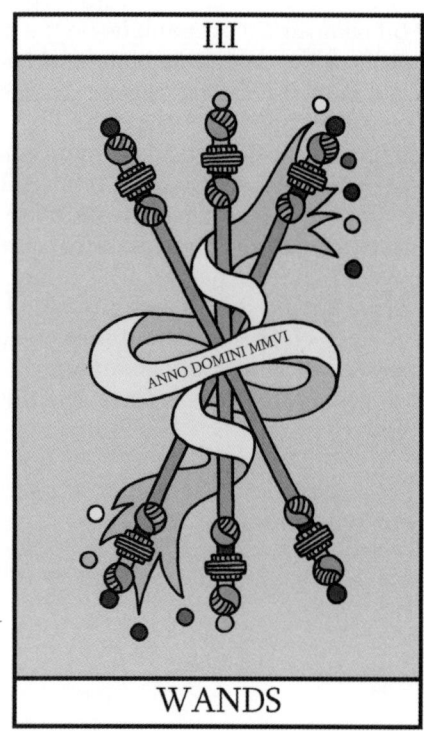

III Wands
The Lord of Established Strength

NUMERICAL VALUE	3
ELEMENT	Fire
TETRAGRAMMATRON	Yod (Primal Energy)
LIFE ASPECT	Career and Enterprise
ASTROLOGICAL ASSOCIATIONS	Leo, Aries, Sagittarius

Guideline Divinatory Meanings:

Keywords (Upright): Dreams coming true, past efforts, worthwhile decision making, travel, growth

Upright – Dreams that turn into reality through circumstance and being in the right place at the right time. Successful ventures launched, inspiration, and original ideas. Strength coming from successful enterprise due to the courage of one's convictions. Plans and ventures that are moving ahead.

The Three of Wands is a card that is symbolic of decisions that have been made and now those decisions are bearing fruit. It is a card of happiness and optimism. As Wands are generally associated with travel anyway, then you may find that you have some business-related trips. If you are feeling anxious about anything at the moment, then with this card in your spread, you should find that your worries begin to decrease. You have already done all of the groundwork necessary to put your plans into action, now is the time to enjoy the rewards. In terms of relationships then this card is indicative of growth and sometimes some travel may be starred.

- Plans and ventures moving on; keep on going, you can't go wrong.

Keywords (Reversed): Plans not put into action, retreat into fantasy, propaganda, unrealistic goals

Ill Dignified or Reversed – Failure to put plans into action. Striving for unattainable goals. Lack of communication between dreams and reality. Issues relating to a promising looking enterprise. Great plans that may not come to fruition. A retreat from reality into fantasy.

The Three of Wands reversed suggests that a promising venture may not bear fruit. Traditionally, threes are all about growth, and if your three Wands tip over in a breeze to the reversed position, then they aren't going to produce anything particularly fruitful. The Three of Wands upright stars travel, so in the reversed position, you could find journeys delayed. There is a sense with this card that projects may prove disappointing, especially if they involve grandiose plans with unrealistic goals. The best way to deal with all of this is to lower expectations, keep focused, and avoid daydreaming on the job.

- Even if it's a poor crop, don't give up, you must not stop.

IV Wands
The Lord of Perfected Work

NUMERICAL VALUE	4
ELEMENT	Fire
TETRAGRAMMATRON	Yod (Primal Energy)
LIFE ASPECT	Career and Enterprise
ASTROLOGICAL ASSOCIATIONS	Leo, Aries, Sagittarius

Guideline Divinatory Meanings:

Keywords (Upright): Firm foundations, consolidation, harmony, prosperity and peace

Upright – The fruits of one's labour, hard work resulting in the successful completion of a project. This is the card of the professional man/woman: an innovator or renowned designer. The establishment of culture, refinement, charm, attractiveness, and splendor. Depending upon the surrounding cards, there is a possibility of romance.

The Four of Wands is symbolic of the laying down of firm foundations for the future. It is a card of looking back and admiring the fruits of one's labour. This card is indicative of the completion of projects and whatever has been established is worthwhile and should be enjoyed. Consolidation is a good descriptive term for the meaning of this card, particularly if two or more fours appear in a reading because this suggests the realization of one's dreams and fulfillment of your ambitions. With this card in your spread, you may find that relationships move to a deeper commitment or will acquire solid foundations. If you are considering the purchase of a property, then now would be a good time to give this serious thought; and if you have had any money worries lately, then this is a good card, as it can indicate monetary success.

- The best harmony and delight you've ever known, brought straight into the heart of your home.
- The "Marriage" card.

Keywords (Reversed): Unorthodox happiness, life ruled by the superfluous, innate snobbery, tensions in business hinders progress

Ill Dignified or Reversed – Happiness that is unorthodox in nature. A life ruled by superfluous and artificial constraints and rules. Tradition which leads to innate snobbery and superiority. Exceptional and profound reliance upon ceremony, decorum and routine. A period of respite before successfully concluding a project.

The Four of Wands reversed is all about a lack of stability. If you imagine the Four of Wands as four supporting pillars, it appears that when they reverse and fall to the ground, all of the support has gone. The Four of Wands reversed does not provide a firm foundation. What this may mean in a spread is that you need to avoid taking anything for granted. Try to look deeper into all situations and free yourself from the superficial. Sometimes the Four of Wands in its upright position can signify marriage, so there is a warning here to ensure that your relationship is on a firm footing before jumping in and tying the knot. In a partnership, generally, there is a suggestion that because the foundations were never firm, then the intensity between the couple will not develop. Do not let the falling Wands lock you into a prison of unnecessary ceremony and routine; and don't let the idea that just because you follow well-worn tradition this makes you a better person. Indeed the Four of Wands reversed is all about lack of foundation and sometimes it is necessary to reassess priorities in order to be more grounded.

- Firm foundations turn to dust; make them solid – this is a must.

Hidden Meaning: The Four of Wands with the Nine of Cups signifies a dream or wish come true.

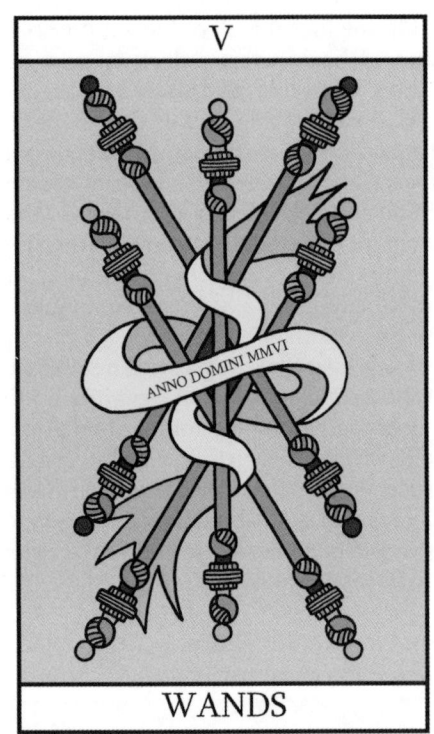

V Wands
The Lord of Strife

NUMERICAL VALUE	5
ELEMENT	Fire
TETRAGRAMMATRON	Yod (Primal Energy)
LIFE ASPECT	Career and Enterprise
ASTROLOGICAL ASSOCIATIONS	Leo, Aries, Sagittarius

Guideline Divinatory Meanings:

Keywords (Upright): Trials and tribulations, irritations, clashes and some conflicts, change

Upright – Problems and possibly upheaval that simply cannot be avoided. Minor irritations may also occur, but whatever the circumstances, i.e., tests, opposition, trouble, strife; great mental agility, and the use of one's inner mental resources will be needed to triumph. Success can be achieved, but only through relentless hard work.

The Five of Wands is a card that can bring with it a "spoke in the wheel of life," or a "fly in the ointment," so to speak. When things are going smoothly, often there is something that comes along to challenge the status quo, and the Five of Wands warns of this. In traditional imagery, five wands or sticks are seen clashing together and this could mean the clashing of personalities, or conflicts that begin to arise. If you are a member of a group or team, you may find that this group is not necessarily working together at its best. However, it could also mean that you are wrestling with your inner emotions because of too many demands on your time. In a relationship, you need to be careful of falling into a pattern of leading separate lives and watch out for any conflicts. Although this card can put the break on the smooth running of your life, problems can be overcome, but it will take effort on your part.

- Struggle and strife is now rife; finish the argument and get on with your life.
- A "Discussion" card.

Keywords (Reversed): Avoidable legal wrangles, unsettled business practices

Ill Dignified or Reversed – Trickery, deception, acrimony, upset. Litigation and legal wrangles. Spiteful conversation and unnecessary competitiveness.

The Five of Wands reversed is like its upright self, also a card of change. In its upright position, the change is not always necessarily good and can be described as a "fly in the ointment." The upright card also symbolizes struggles, irritations, and clashes. Logically then, it could be expected that in its reverse position, a more positive outlook could be anticipated. However, this is not necessarily the case. This card is more symbolic of someone who gives up their struggle before it has even begun. By simply eyeing up the competition, they have decided that the competitors are already better than themselves so they decide that they are already beaten. The way to avoid this is not to deceive yourself into thinking that you can't win the battle. Nothing is ever completely over, until (as the popular saying goes), "the fat lady sings." When all of the Wands have fallen to the floor in the reversed position, there may be wrangles, spiteful conversations, and maybe even some upset. However, if you persevere and sift through the debris of Wands on the floor, and without giving in, you will find a positive way forward.

- The battle is not already won; don't give up before you've begun.

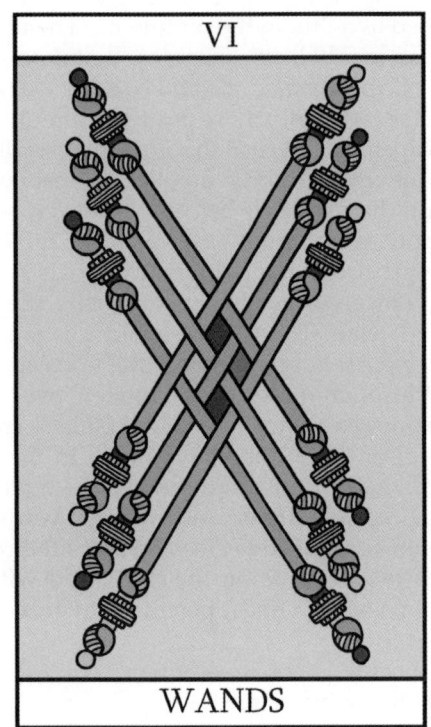

VI Wands
The Lord of Victory

NUMERICAL VALUE	6
ELEMENT	Fire
TETRAGRAMMATRON	Yod (Primal Energy)
LIFE ASPECT	Career and Enterprise
ASTROLOGICAL ASSOCIATIONS	Leo, Aries, Sagittarius

Guideline Divinatory Meanings:

Keywords (Upright): Adaptability, public acclaim, success, progress, fulfilment, stability

Upright – The arrival of fantastic good news. Success and great public acclaim gained through hard work and effort. Hopefulness and satisfaction in what has been achieved. The surmounting of obstacles through tact and diplomacy rather than use of force. Victory and triumph.

The Six of Wands is an excellent card to have in your spread, especially if you haven't been having the best time lately. This is a card where you will realize exactly what it is that has been bothering you and exactly how to fix the problem. It will be almost like having a *Eureka* moment. This is a card that symbolizes both victory and gains. Your past efforts will be rewarded and any legal issues may be favorably resolved. Progress is starred with this card. Relationships are also well starred, as this card suggests that you and your partner have similar aims and objectives; therefore, a new level of commitment may be in the cards because of this. Your confidence should grow and so too your adaptability to any changing events or difficulties.

- This is a game that you can win, just as long as you don't give in.
- A "Victory" card.

Keywords (Reversed): Indecision, seek moderation, fear of surreptitious activity, delayed news, focus energies to prevent failure

Ill Dignified or Reversed – Indecision, fear that one's enemies are engaging in surreptitious activity. Fear about the outcome of a situation. Delayed news or rewards, or possibly even unwelcome news.

The Six of Wands reversed is not a card of public acclaim and success as is its upright self. In fact, the reversed card might even suggest the opposite of success, but the meaning may be a little more subtle than that. For example, imagine writing a book only to discover that someone failed to mention that you were the author, or winning a lottery only to find that there was no prize. There is still satisfaction in actually achieving something, but the just rewards don't seem to appear. Success as a whole may still be possible, but there may be a few delays and obstacles in achieving it. When the Six of Wands fall down from their upright position, it will take a strong focus to reassemble them all again, but this is far from impossible. Stay focused, don't worry about underhanded dealings and don't worry about outcomes. In a relationship, don't expect too much from a partner at this time.

- If the reward is less than expected, try not to feel too dejected.

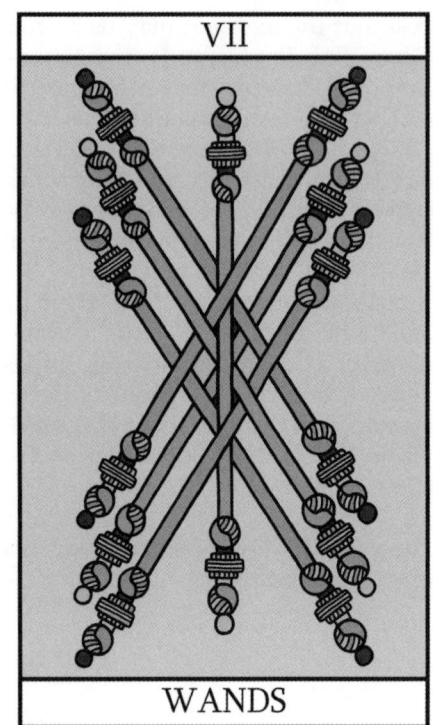

VII Wands
The Lord of Valor

NUMERICAL VALUE	7
ELEMENT	Fire
TETRAGRAMMATRON	Yod (Primal Energy)
LIFE ASPECT	Career and Enterprise
ASTROLOGICAL ASSOCIATIONS	Leo, Aries, Sagittarius

Guideline Divinatory Meanings:

Keywords (Upright): Taking charge, taking the reins, refusing to give in, valor, completion, difficult negotiations

Upright – Successful advancement. A time of great opportunity requiring much skill, courage and determination in order to succeed. Strength of nerve, great fortitude and courage in the face of hardship. An indication that success may be achieved through sustained effort. Indicates strong and powerful competition.

The Seven of Wands is a card that is very similar in meaning to the Five of Wands in that it signifies a "spoke in the wheel." You may find that up to now projects have been successful, but currently certain situations or other people are making things difficult. Your plans may no longer be acceptable to others and this could place you in a somewhat more competitive environment. However, you need to see the fruits of your labor and the way this can be achieved is through courage and sustained hard work and effort. This card can also suggest that some people may envy what you have achieved to date and this must be addressed. You must find a way to take control, move yourself into a position where you are in charge. In business, this card is symbolic of competition, and in a relationship, as the relationship deepens, so too may the challenges within it. The message here is to be aware of what is going on around you and do not lose sight of your goals, as the achievement of your heart's desire will be well worth the effort.

- Many problems in the way; sort them now, to clear your day.
- The "Self Protection" card and "Standing your Ground" card.

Keywords (Reversed): Indecision jeopardizes any challenges, opportunities lost, giving in

Ill Dignified or Reversed – Indecision and retreat. Lack of decisiveness that hinders the challenge. Opportunities lost through hesitation. Giving in just as the end was in sight. Depending upon surrounding cards, a turning away from success due to fears of responsibility.

The Seven of Wands reversed is very similar to the Five of Wands reversed. Just like the Five of Wands reversed, the Seven reversed is all about giving up. Imagine this card turned on its head and being buried under a mound of Wands, this would be enough to rattle anyone. The Seven of Wands upright is all about holding your ground and not giving in. It is about skillfully negotiating your way around any difficult situations to succeed in the face of adversity. However, the Seven reversed is about not having the stomach to do this. It is about feeling that something is worth fighting for, but the willpower and energy are simply not there for the querent to stand up and be counted. Now would be a good time to limit any restrictions that you may be placing on yourself. If someone insists you are wrong, but you know you are right, now may be the time to say so. Decisive action and a belief that you can succeed will help you when this card pops up in a spread. The weight of those Wands on top of you might be quite hard to bear, but don't forget, you can always tunnel your way out.

- It is not the time to give in; concede now, and you won't win.

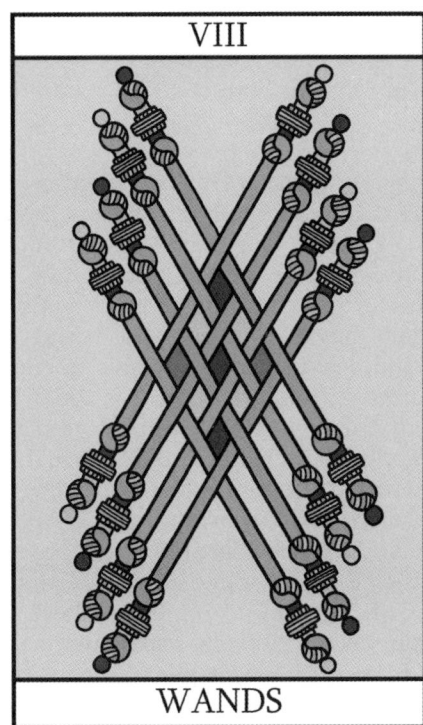

VIII Wands
The Lord of Swiftness

NUMERICAL VALUE	8
ELEMENT	Fire
TETRAGRAMMATRON	Yod (Primal Energy)
LIFE ASPECT	Career and Enterprise
ASTROLOGICAL ASSOCIATIONS	Leo, Aries, Sagittarius

Guideline Divinatory Meanings:

Keywords (Upright): Enthusiasm, strength, hope, positive action, personal power

Upright – Understanding and harmony. The time and conditions are right to facilitate success. A process of speeding-up and an end to delays. A time for "grasping the nettle," taking the initiative or taking charge. This card also indicates important journeys, correspondence, and favorable news. A card of hope.

The Eight of Wands is a card that is symbolic of having the drive, determination, and energy to move forward and make things happen. It is a card about rolling up your sleeves and "getting stuck in," particularly if the situation is not necessarily the easiest to manage. As with the whole suit of Wands, travel is starred and this may even be abroad. If you have been waiting for an answer to any correspondence, then this should arrive shortly. This is a card of free-flowing energy that seems to know no bounds and with it should come advancement and change that is positive in nature. However, because events around you may be fast moving and change from minute to minute or hour to hour, then beware of any ill-considered or hasty decisions at this time. In a relationship, the Eight of Wands is a very good card to have in your spread, as it suggests that you are giving each other just the right amount of space so that everyone feels comfortable. Generally, the Eight of Wands is a good card, so make sure you harness all your energy and channel it in the right direction.

- Grasp the nettle and success will flow; climb up that ladder and off you go.
- A card of "new faces, new places."

Keywords (Reversed): Disputes, wasted effort, silly actions, cancelled journeys, rash actions, think before acting

Ill Dignified or Reversed – Disputes and disagreements. Great effort and a driving force that is totally wasted through the running out of steam. Silly, spontaneous actions. Cancelled journeys. Sometimes redundancy or work-related issues. Jumping in both feet first before testing the water.

The Eight of Wands reversed, when seen as a blockage card, can symbolize things getting in the way or even a rug being pulled from under foot. If you imagine the Eight of Wands upright as a structure to climb up to reach your goals, then when the card reverses, the Wands fall to the ground, leaving nothing stable to climb up. When approaching a ladder, it is important to ensure that its rungs will support your weight before leaping on the first step. So when this card reversed turns up in a spread, it is really important to look before you leap into anything – plan any actions carefully. Relationship issues are starred with this card reversed and any travel plans may be delayed. The key to remember here is that even though your metaphorical ladder may have collapsed, you still have a pile of Wands to stack up to help form the basis of your ascent again; just ensure that the structure you build is solid.

- Always look before you leap, as bad decisions are yours to keep.

IX Wands
The Lord of Great Strength

NUMERICAL VALUE	9
ELEMENT	Fire
TETRAGRAMMATRON	Yod (Primal Energy)
LIFE ASPECT	Career and Enterprise
ASTROLOGICAL ASSOCIATIONS	Leo, Aries, Sagittarius

Guideline Divinatory Meanings:

Keywords (Upright): Reassessment, determination, courage, illumination, happiness, profitable friendship

Upright – Order, discipline, an unassailable position. Any opposition will be defeated. Courage in the face of attack or adversity and a stability that cannot be removed. Good health.

The Nine of Wands is a card all about moving yourself into a good, unassailable position. Think of this card like moving up the rungs of a huge ladder: You are nearing the top, but you are becoming increasingly weary as you move toward your goal, i.e., the top of the ladder. The message that this card brings is that the energy and drive and determination are all there, but you must carry on. This card is also symbolic of completion; if you have a number of incomplete projects, then now may be the time to complete them. Turn any delays to your advantage and keep pushing yourself forward. In terms of a relationship, if you have been hurt in the past, this could be hampering your ability to commit to your present one. Generally, this is a positive card, and as long as you continue pushing forward with drive and determination, things should come to fruition.

- When you make your last stand, be sure to know help is at hand.
- The "Last Stand" card.

Keywords (Reversed): Lack of give and take, business success depends upon prudence, delays, health-related issues

Ill Dignified or Reversed – Lack or inability to give and take. Impractical projects are destined to fail. Delays and disarray. Card could indicate possible health-related issues. A secure position that is no longer. Personality flaws.

The Nine of Wands reversed is a card symbolic of getting so far with something, but not being able to make that final push for completion. In its upright position the Nine of Wands can be likened to the "Last Stand" card. It's a case of being aware that the cavalry is around the corner, but having the drive and determination to hang on till they arrive. However, in its reversed position, the cavalry either doesn't turn up or you can't hang in any longer till they do. It could be that a project or situation has become too impractical or too big to handle. It is possible that this may be having a negative impact health wise. The best advice when this card turns up reversed is to take care of yourself and try not to take on board too much. Look to the positive in that the cavalry will eventually arrive and it's just a case of having the necessary faith and determination to carry on and see things through.

- When you fear you are all alone, you're quite right – you're on your own.

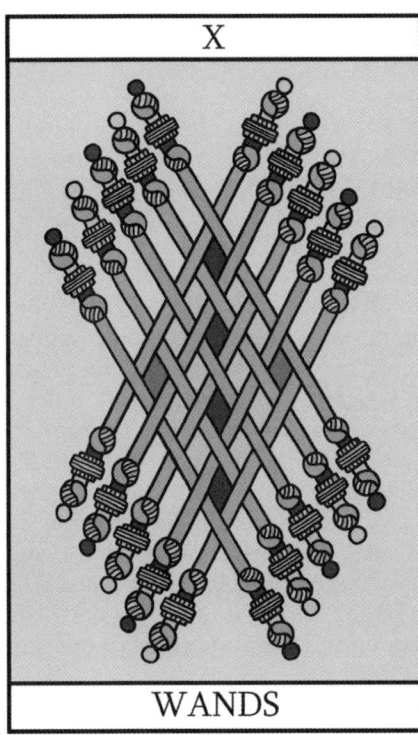

X Wands
The Lord of Oppression

NUMERICAL VALUE	10
ELEMENT	Fire
TETRAGRAMMATRON	Yod (Primal Energy)
LIFE ASPECT	Career and Enterprise
ASTROLOGICAL ASSOCIATIONS	Leo, Aries, Sagittarius

Guideline Divinatory Meanings:

Keywords (Upright): Completion, pressure, burden, over-ambition

Upright – Conduct that is honourable. Great good fortune that is now a burden due to its demanding nature and demands on time. Diseconomies of scale in business. A successful pastime that can no longer be administered by its creator. Lack of social life due to the demands of a project, job, or overtime.

The Ten of Wands is a card that suggests that now you have climbed to the top of your ladder, you may be running out of steam – both physically, mentally, and spiritually. Energy at the beginning of your project, challenge, and/or life journey is running out. Although you may have achieved your aims or ambition, the success and the extra responsibility that comes with it may be becoming burdensome. For example, if you have just had a promotion or you are now the boss, although this in itself may be great, the added weight of responsibility brings its own set of problems. Now might be a good time to delegate and share your burdens until you have "re-charged your batteries" and are feeling more refreshed and confident to resume things as normal. Take care not to overdo things and try to share the workload.

- Now you're at the top of your tree, shoulder the burden of success, and be the best you can be.

Keywords (Reversed): Alteration in working conditions, a change in status, jealousy may fuel an effort to spoil things

Ill Dignified or Reversed – Efforts to spoil the pleasures and affairs of others because of jealousy. Disloyalty. An inability to delegate in a job leading to unnecessary stress. Lies and deceit used to upset others.

The Ten of Wands reversed may be symbolic of shirking responsibility or not being able to successfully delegate the responsibility that leads to undue stress. In its upright position, the Ten of Wands is about achieving one's goals and being successful. The down side of the upright card, is that with all of those Wands carried on your back, representing the extra worries and responsibilities that success can sometimes bring, there is a sense of being weighed down by it all. It is the burden of success, if you like. When this card reverses, the Wands are tossed to the floor, or in other words, all burdens and responsibility are removed and thrown to the floor. It is like a throwing down of one's worries, burdens, responsibilities, and woes that success has brought. It may be that a promotion or a pay rise are very welcome, but not so the extra duties they bring. Unfortunately, someone has to pick up the pieces. Therefore, instead of simply walking away from it all, it is better to work with colleagues, to share the workload. This is to avoid being labeled someone who shirks their responsibility. This card reversed suggests that there may be a need to cut down on your workload, otherwise your emotional needs may be overlooked. The key here is to delegate responsibility, ask a number of friends, relations, or colleagues to each pick up one of the fallen Wands. In that way, everyone fairly shares the load.

- Now's the time to delegate, share the work, before it's too late.

Page Wands
The Princess of the Shining Flame
The Rose of the Palace of Fire

NUMERICAL VALUE	7
ELEMENT	Fire
ELEMENTAL NAME	Earth of Fire
TETRAGRAMMATRON	Yod (Primal Energy)
HAIR COLOR	Red or Blond
EYE COLOR	Blue
LIFE ASPECT	Career and Enterprise
ASTROLOGICAL ASSOCIATIONS	Leo, Aries, Sagittarius

Guideline Divinatory Meanings:

Keywords (Upright): Faithfulness, a postman, a messenger, inspiration, creativity, a youth of Sagittarian temperament

Upright – A trustworthy, reliable young person, with an inborn desire to bring happiness, excitement, and light to those around. This person is a messenger of good news and witty gossip. A person who is faithful in service to superiors.

The Page of Wands, as with all of the Court Cards, can be some of the most difficult to read in a spread. This is because not only can they symbolize certain events or issues relating to your life, just as the other cards do, they can also symbolize a person. Pages are linked to children, so if you have any in your life at the moment, then you may recognize one who is always active and energetic and often comes in late from play. This child can be male or female and is always full of fun and likes to be the center of attention. If children do not focus in your life, then this card often symbolizes the receipt of great good news that will cheer you up. A young person may be about to offer you some help and any family issues may be drawing to a close. The Page of Wands is a nice card to have in your spread and can act as the creative spark or flash of inspiration that sets you off to go and learn something new.

- Fair hair, red hair, eyes of blue, someone's out there, with lovely news, for you.

Keywords (Reversed): Petulance, gossip, rumors, a questioning of trust

Ill Dignified or Reversed – Honest qualities, that may turn to petulance. Someone who believes they are trustworthy, but all the time being unfaithful. A person unable to keep a confidence, someone who betrays trust and spreads gossip. The card can also indicate journeys that are delayed or a change of address.

The Page of Wands reversed signifies someone who possesses completely different traits from those of his upright counterpart. In the upright position, Pages generally signify youngish children and the Page of Wands is usually one who is fun loving and helpful. However, once he is turned on his head, he becomes somewhat petulant, and, at his worst, he can even be a bit of a bully. Normally, the Page of Wands upright signifies good news, but when upside down, this is not the case. Any news received may be more like a rejection, "Dear John," or a general letdown letter, but on the plus side, it may just be delayed good news. In his reversed position, he is not particularly helpful with travel either, as when he is upside down and laid on the floor, he symbolically blocks the way, causing travel plans to be put on hold. But remember, children are usually small, and, therefore, to win with this card, you may need to pick him up and simply move him out of the way.

- Eyes of blue, hair red and fair, open the letter if you dare.

Knight Wands

The Lord of the Flame and the Lightning
The King of the Spirits of Fire

NUMERICAL VALUE	4
ELEMENT	Fire
ELEMENTAL NAME	Fire of Fire
TETRAGRAMMATRON	Yod (Primal Energy)
HAIR COLOR	Blond
EYE COLOR	Blue or Gray
LIFE ASPECT	Career and Enterprise
ASTROLOGICAL ASSOCIATIONS	Leo, Aries, Sagittarius

Guideline Divinatory Meanings:

Keywords (Upright): Travel, possible emigration, swift decisions, thoughts of business, advantageous thinking

Upright – A lover of action, this is the card of someone who has a well-liked, energetic, confident, but sometimes unpredictable nature. He has an engaging temperament and his actions, sometimes a little swift, do tend to make sense with hindsight.

The Knight of Wands, when representing a person, is symbolic of a teen who likes to live life in the "fast lane." He/she really enjoys fast cars and parties and loves to live life to the full. This teen, however, may have a very fiery and forthright nature, but on all counts he/she will be very keen to get in amongst all of the action. However, in general, the focus of The Knight of Wands is on decision making and certainly some changes are starred. As with the whole suit of Wands, travel is also on the cards. It is possible that you may also find yourself changing jobs, moving home, or even embarking upon a new relationship. Certainly, if you have been somewhat bored with life at present, all of that is now about to change. This card has even been linked to emigration.

- Fair hair, eyes of blue, this person's swift actions, could impact on you.
- A card of "Jack be nimble, Jack be quick, Jack jump over the candle stick."

Keywords (Reversed): Delayed travel, change, an enthusiastic person who enjoys discord, thoughts opposed to business interests

Ill Dignified or Reversed – The Knight of Wands reversed has enthusiasm that is so great it becomes at odds with those around. He or she is someone who enjoys discord, arguments, strife, and trouble just for the sake of it and actively seeks to cause it. This card may also indicate delayed journeys.

The Knight of Wands reversed – just like his/her younger sister or brother, the Page of Wands reversed, can be a bit of a bully, too. He/she is someone who likes to be the center of attention and in among all of the action. However, he/she prefers it if the action in question is more discord and strife than party atmosphere. This person paints himself/herself as rather an intolerant figure and is very at home in the middle of an argument. Like a younger reversed counterpart, he/she can symbolize delayed travel, but the main trait is to make trouble just for the sake of it. This Knight also finds commitments difficult to make, so he wouldn't star very well in a relationship spread. Indeed he is like a bear with a sore head when he is upside down and reversed; mainly because his horse falls on top of him. When he shows up in a spread, just remember that this person can be helped back onto the metaphorical horse, so that he can ride back out of your life as quickly as he crashed in.

- Fair hair, eyes of blue, watch out for this person, they may bully you.

Queen Wands
The Queen of the Thrones of Flame

NUMERICAL VALUE	4
ELEMENT	Fire
ELEMENTAL NAME	Water of Fire
TETRAGRAMMATRON	Yod (Primal Energy)
HAIR COLOR	Red or Blond
EYE COLOR	Blue or Brown
LIFE ASPECT	Career and Enterprise
ASTROLOGICAL ASSOCIATIONS	Leo, Aries, Sagittarius

Guideline Divinatory Meanings:

Keywords (Upright): Forging a career possibly in acting, drama, or leadership, a fun-loving woman, a woman of Leo temperament

Upright – A lady of the manor either living in or loving the country. A very generous, capable, and fair person, especially in her dealings with people. A woman who is both fertile in mind and body and a home maker. She enjoys social ease due to her charm and is protective towards those in her circle. The card may also indicate the success of a project.

The Queen of Wands is a card that symbolizes strong, positive, and forthright women who are usually over the age of 22. With this card in your spread, it is possible that you may encounter a very vibrant, friendly, and fun-loving woman. This lady may be very good and at ease at social gatherings and she may even hold the key to your future business success. This card is also symbolic of business opportunities and the success of projects through your own inner strength and resources. It is a great card for anyone who would like to have a career in acting, drama, or some job involving strong leadership. You may also find that you want to make a trip or go on a journey. It is also possible that now is the time to lay down some firm foundations for your career.

- Hair red or blond, eyes brown or blue, this lady is always generous with you.

Keywords (Reversed): A bitter lady with a harsh, cruel dry sense of humor, envy, relationship issues, dishonesty

Ill Dignified or Reversed – A person who has a tendency to dominate or to be bitter; an envious, matriarchal and overbearing woman. A person who has a cruel very dry sense of humor and tends to imagine people are out to get her, even though malice was never present or intended.

The Queen of Wands reversed is a complete polar opposite from her upright self. If Queens in general are the driving forces behind making things happen, then this upside down "topsy-turvy" lady is finding it hard to complete anything at the moment. She seems as if she is totally unable to be helpful and unable to do her job. Instead of her fun loving and friendly attitude when she is upright, the bang on the head from her fall upside down has left her a more bitter and shallow person. She has now become someone that you do not want to anger. She will ensure that anyone who crosses her will be ostracized from her group. Her dry sense of humor becomes increasingly cruel and her paranoia increases. She imagines that people are plotting her downfall, when actually treason was never on the cards. In a relationship, she warns of fickle behavior and infidelity. Therefore, when the Queen of Wands reversed appears in a spread, it may be wise to simply offer her a metaphorical bandage for her head and an aspirin to ease her pain and then send her happily on her way.

- Hair red or blond, eyes blue or brown, this lady certainly will make you frown.

King Wands
The Prince of the Chariot of Fire

NUMERICAL VALUE	4
ELEMENT	Fire
ELEMENTAL NAME	Air of Fire
TETRAGRAMMATRON	Yod (Primal Energy)
HAIR COLOR	Red or Blond
EYE COLOR	Gray or Hazel
LIFE ASPECT	Career and Enterprise
ASTROLOGICAL ASSOCIATIONS	Leo, Aries, Sagittarius

Guideline Divinatory Meanings:

Keywords (Upright): Grand plans, taking charge, wise and helpful mentors, a man of Aries temperament

Upright – A charming, responsible, loyal, entertaining, witty, honest, conscientious, and generous person. A lover of home and family life. A very passionate and virile man who is good at moral support and encouragement. When pushed or provoked, he acts without hesitation, but can sometimes find this hard as he can often see both sides of an argument.

The King of Wands is symbolic of a very forthright and honest, trustworthy man who is well disposed towards you. This person will probably be over 30 years of age. Also, if you have any problems or troubles at the moment, then the King of Wands represents someone who is very fair-minded, non-judgmental, straight-forward, and energetic coming to your aid. However, as well as a person, the King of Wands symbolizes the beginning of something very grand; for example, you may be thinking of planning a big trip, changing your career, or even seeing yourself moving into politics. This is a card of big and grand plans, ideas, taking charge of your life, and ultimately turning your dreams into reality.

- Eyes gray or hazel, hair red or fair, when you need him, he's always there.

Keywords (Reversed): An inability to understand the viewpoint of others, bigotry, prejudice, ruthlessness

Ill Dignified or Reversed – He has an inability to understand or appreciate another's point of view, particularly if they are coming from a lower moral standpoint than his own. He is intolerant, narrow minded, and a bigot with deep prejudices. He has a ruthless streak and cares little for the feelings of others.

The King of Wands reversed becomes an altogether formidable character, but not in a positive sense. Just like his Queen, when he reverses and falls upside down, he too receives a bang on his head from his throne. Unfortunately though for him, it's a double whammy, as he receives a second blow from his Wand as well. This has left him displaying some very unpleasant characteristics. Instead of the very forthright, honest, and trustworthy man that was well disposed to those around him, he has become a megalomaniac! He would probably feel at home with the very worst of tyrants. Ivan the Terrible probably would seem like a pussycat next to this ruler. Reversed, he is the type of ruthless leader who would employ all manner of unorthodox methods to keep his subjects down. He expects his followers to treat him as a god-like figure and to worship and adore him at all costs. "Woe betide" anyone who does not share his point of view either publicly or privately. Indeed, privately his secret police would soon know if any rebellion was in the offing. Not only does the King of Wands reversed appear as a wholly negative character, he also serves to block any creative inspiration at this time. The best way to defeat this card in a spread is to metaphorically help him back onto his thrown, then make a quick exit for the door.

- Eyes gray or hazel, hair fair or red, he's a character full of dread.

Ace Cups
The Root of the Powers of Water

NUMERICAL VALUE	5
SEASON	Summer
DIRECTION	West
ELEMENT	Water
TETRAGRAMMATRON	Heh (Energy into Form)
LIFE ASPECT	Emotions
ASTROLOGICAL ASSOCIATIONS	Pisces, Cancer, Scorpio

Guideline Divinatory Meanings:

Keywords (Upright): New beginnings, fulfillment, joy, letters from loved ones, emotional talk

Upright – Faithfulness, fertility, joy, love. The commencement of creative or artistic projects. All the positive powers of the unconscious mind.

The Ace of Cups symbolizes that there are opportunities out there to bring happiness into your life. Now might be a good time for emotional and spiritual development. You may find that ideas are starting to flow as the Ace is symbolic of that creative spark or attraction between people. You may also be finding that somewhere deep inside you new thoughts are beginning to emerge and you may be thinking about some form of psychic development. This is a positive card if you have just started a new relationship and can indicate that things generally look promising in that area.

- With feelings of joy deep within your heart, you are ready to tackle any new start.

Keywords (Reversed): Negative changes, a time of mental or physical unfruitfulness, faithlessness

Ill Dignified or Reversed – The card is symbolic of negative changes, possibly a time of barrenness, which can be either of a physical or mental nature. Love issues, stagnation, upset and possibly loss of faith.

The Ace of Cups reversed is symbolic of a cup that is not just half empty, this vessel is positively dry. As the Ace of Cups reverses, it turns upside down and all of its positive energy spills out onto the floor. Generally, Aces are symbolic of starting something new. When the Ace of Cups upright shows up in a spread, it is a very positive card that suggests that whatever new is entering your life will be emotionally as well as physically rewarding. The Ace of Cups lights up all of your senses. However, in its reversed position, the Ace cup is empty and its creative spark extinguished by its own creative juices that have spilled on the floor. Therefore, when this reversed card shows up in a spread, it may indicate a period of instability, which in turn may be a cause for anxiety. In relationships, generally, there is a caution about false friends and lovers. Now may not be the best time for starting new projects. This cup needs to be filled up again before it can work in your favor. Do not lose faith; find a tap, fill the cup, and drink the fresh water.

- Sometimes change is not the best, keep the faith and you'll be blessed.

II Cups
The Lord of Love

NUMERICAL VALUE	2
ELEMENT	Water
TETRAGRAMMATRON	Heh (Energy into Form)
LIFE ASPECT	Emotions
ASTROLOGICAL ASSOCIATIONS	Pisces, Cancer, Scorpio

Guideline Divinatory Meanings:

Keywords (Upright): Soul mates, decisions, love, affection, passion, revelation, romantic impulses, love of home, reciprocated love

Upright – Affection, love, the beginnings of a new romance, partnership, or friendship. Emotional affinity, sympathy, joyous harmony, the reconciliation of opposites in mutual trust. Resolved differences.

The Two of Cups is a card about the recognition of love. It is about gazing into someone's eyes and realizing that you have made a deep and lasting connection, or even found your soul mate. This card is about an affinity with someone on all levels and the simple union of two people who are very much in love. If you are already in a relationship, then you may feel that now is the time to move towards a deeper commitment or even marriage.

- Two persons together in harmony, it's definitely where they ought to be.
- A "Romance" card.

Keywords (Reversed): Impulsive love, secret romances revealed, mistrust in personal relationships, dissent

Ill Dignified or Reversed – Relationship issues. Sometimes separation, dissent, divorce, deceit, or unfaithfulness in a personal relationship. Misunderstandings and quarrels, love not returned.

The Two of Cups reversed: Instead of the union of something, it is the pulling apart of it. In its upright position, the Two of Cups is one of the most romantic cards in the pack. Relationships are well starred and any love given is reciprocated. In its reverse position, the cups fall apart from each other; they are no longer held together. In its extreme form, relating to a relationship, this reversed card suggests that there may be some form of breakup. At the very least, it suggests that the partners are moving in different directions. There may be relationship issues and possibly arguments. This card also warns of unfaithfulness and possibly lies in a personal relationship. For this reason, it is doubly important to ensure to tread carefully and not make any rash decisions that may be regretted in the future. In a metaphorical sense, these two upturned cups need to be brought back together again before harmony and balance can be restored.

- When love becomes torn apart, team up again, for a new start.

III Cups
The Lord of Abundance

NUMERICAL VALUE	3
ELEMENT	Water
TETRAGRAMMATRON	Heh (Energy into Form)
LIFE ASPECT	Emotions
ASTROLOGICAL ASSOCIATIONS	Pisces, Cancer, Scorpio

Guideline Divinatory Meanings:

Keywords (Upright): Growth, celebrations, family gatherings, something conceived out of love that is coming to fruition, romantic activity

Upright – A fortunate end to a valued project or venture. A birth, possibly physical, but may mean the birth of a new project instead. Great happiness as the result of a marriage or a birth. Something coming to fruition that was conceived out of love. A card of abundant fertility, trust harmony, maternity, and the healing of ills. Possibly a celebration.

The Three of Cups is a card of celebration, often family celebrations such as births and marriages. You may well be finding at the moment that your past efforts are beginning to produce the desired results and you may well be feeling full of optimism, joy, and determination. There may also be a tendency at this time to let your heart be ruled by your head, and your emotions will play a large part in actions or decision making that you may be undertaking at the moment. This card is also symbolic of better health and it can indicate that any past problems are about to be resolved. For those in a relationship, the Three of Cups may signify a choice between a number of partners or relationships, but it can also mean a successful reunion between people.

- Everything turns out superbly in the end. Nothing is broken, nothing to mend.
- The "Celebration" card.

Keywords (Reversed): Unbridled emotions, selfishness, self indulgence, health-related issues, a danger of over indulgence

Ill Dignified or Reversed – Self indulgence to excess. Selfishness and sensuality. Relationship issues. Loveless sex, unbridled passion, shortages, health issues possibly associated with smoking or over-eating. Promiscuity and obesity.

The Three of Cups reversed is like a celebration turned sour. There may very well have been a party, but all of the guests got drunk. Imagine Three Cups of red wine falling onto a white carpet. The excessive liquid saturates the carpet's fabric to the point that a cloth or mop won't wipe it up. This is enough to leave anyone feeling somewhat defeated. When the Three of Cups appears in a spread, then it is a time to guard against excess. Try to avoid any forms of over indulgence, whether it is in the area of sex, drugs, or rock and roll. Moderation is the key. There is also a suggestion of selfishness and meanness of spirit with this card reversed. This kind of behavior can have a really negative impact on any relationships, so a more generous attitude should be favored. At the end of the day, it might be worth giving up that metaphorical last bottle of white wine, to throw on the red wine that spilled on the carpet. This way there may still be a wet carpet, but at least the stains will be avoided.

- When your cup is sure to overflow, maybe now is the time to go. When everything begins to taste too sweet, you know your time is now complete.

IV Cups
The Lord of Blended Pleasure

NUMERICAL VALUE	4
ELEMENT	Water
TETRAGRAMMATRON	Heh (Energy into Form)
LIFE ASPECT	Emotions
ASTROLOGICAL ASSOCIATIONS	Pisces, Cancer, Scorpio

Guideline Divinatory Meanings:

Keywords (Upright): Consolidation, boredom, a sense of being stuck in a rut, dissatisfaction, love dominates, a legacy

Upright – Time to re-evaluate an all too familiar environment, dissatisfaction, and boredom. The need to search for a more stimulating way of life. Apathy, dwelling on past experience. Love that turns to familiarity. Happiness that has reached its peak. Possibly the establishment of a family.

The Four of Cups is a card of consolidation, but it is also a card that may mean you are becoming a little bored with a situation that has become all too familiar. Things that perhaps once seemed new and exciting are now beginning to seem worn and outdated. In many respects, this card often goes hand in hand with the old saying: "The grass is greener on the other side." However, the question that you must really ask yourself now is whether or not this is really the case. You may find yourself presented with a number of opportunities, but you need to weigh up all of the pros and cons carefully. The Four of Cups in your spread tends to suggest that the time could be right for making long-term plans and you shouldn't make any rash decisions just because you may be feeling a little bored at the moment.

- When boredom comes, making you feel blue, remember, there's always better things meant for you.

Keywords (Reversed): Tensions in business bar progress, tiredness from excess or health-related issues, swift changes cause concern

Ill Dignified or Reversed – All kinds of excess, health issues, or fatigue as a result of over indulgence. The overturning of a way of life. Rapid change resulting in new anxieties. Excitement for its own sake that brings little or fleeting pleasure. A low boredom threshold.

The Four of Cups reversed symbolizes boredom that has drained away, only to be replaced by complete discontent. Once these cups have fallen to the floor their contents sink into the ground leaving a sense of complete deflation behind. This card reversed suggests that although life may no longer be boring, any rapid change may not bring expected rewards. The advice here is also to steer clear of excess, particularly if you are looking for new experiences as any over indulgence will ultimately lead to health problems. With all four cups on the floor and their contents long absorbed into the ground, now might be the time to carefully reassess any future moves.

- Now's the time to watch your health, over indulgence, catches up by stealth.

Hidden Meaning: The Four of Cups, together with the Devil, may signify an affair with possible emotional manipulation.

V Cups
The Lord of Loss in Pleasure

NUMERICAL VALUE	5
ELEMENT	Water
TETRAGRAMMATRON	Heh (Energy into Form)
LIFE ASPECT	Emotions
ASTROLOGICAL ASSOCIATIONS	Pisces, Cancer, Scorpio

Guideline Divinatory Meanings:

Keywords (Upright): Displeasure, deflated egos, changes, over indulgence strains the wallet

Upright – A need to re-order and re-evaluate priorities. Union and espousal. Sometimes dishonor that may be hard to overcome, loss and defeat. There is a need to curb futile belligerence and accept the inevitable. Worry and regret, broken engagements, and emotional letdowns. Emotional or monetary legacies. All may seem lost but it is not.

The Five of Cups is symbolic of a period when it may seem like your cup is half empty instead of being half full. With the Five of Cups in your spread, you must not focus upon "crying over spilled milk." Instead, you need to look to all of the positives and realize that although the cup may have overturned and thus the milk wet the carpet, at least it didn't break! If someone has upset you, or perhaps you have let yourself down in some way, then you need to realize that dwelling on past situations will not help at all. This card is often associated with bitterness, regrets, and general displeasure. However, it is also an indicator that you really need to let go of any past emotional experiences or situations that may be causing you concern. This is because if you don't, you may miss a genuine opportunity that could be about to present itself. With this card in your spread, try to put the past behind you and focus on the future.

- Although the liquid may be spilled on the ground, there are still opportunities all around.
- A card of "not crying over spilled milk."

Keywords (Reversed): Spend wisely, the overturning of a way of life, some anxieties

Ill Dignified or Reversed – The overturning of a way of life. False starts. Concerns which arrive both unexpectedly and from an unexpected source. Circumstances which leave lovelorn feelings. Worries and anxieties. Learning from the past.

The Five of Cups reversed does not have the same spark of optimism that is present when it appears in its upright position. When the Five of Cups reverses, all of its liquid rushes away; there is no chance that any of the cups remain even half full. Imagine a situation where you settle for second best, but then find out that second best is no longer available, thus leaving you no options at all. This suggests that some kind of change is on the cards. Indeed, it may even symbolize a complete overturning of an existing way of life, which may cause some concern. However, new situations and new ventures not only bring new challenges, but they bring new opportunities as well. Now would be a good time to knock the empty cups out of the way and accept that things have changed and go and find some new opportunities.

- Although your dreams didn't seem to come true, there's lots of great things still waiting for you.

VI Cups
The Lord of Pleasure

NUMERICAL VALUE	6
ELEMENT	Water
TETRAGRAMMATRON	Heh (Energy into Form)
LIFE ASPECT	Emotions
ASTROLOGICAL ASSOCIATIONS	Pisces, Cancer, Scorpio

Guideline Divinatory Meanings:

Keywords (Upright): Harmony, stability, solutions from the past that present themselves in the present, nostalgia, loyalty

Upright – Harmony, past associations have brought present relationships. A sense of the past. Happiness that results from past efforts. Pleasant memories and the realization of a dream. Can also indicate new elements entering one's life that are linked to the past, which will work through the present to create the future.

The six of Cups is a card all about people, places, and memories from the past. It is a card of nostalgia. But it is also a card that symbolizes a period of balance and harmony after any upset that you may have experienced. You may even find that solutions to any current problems may be found by way of a friendly face from the past. In terms of relationships, the Six of Cups can indicate unions that are based on firm and strong foundations although there may be some apprehension surrounding any restrictions that may come from either partner. School reunions, friendly faces from the past, nostalgic moments, and meeting up with old friends and former teachers are all well starred with this card.

- Happiness comes from a tie in the past – keep the memory sweet, it's designed to last.
- The "Nostalgia" card. The old gypsy card that warns against depression, but this depends on other cards.

Keywords (Reversed): Hankering after the past and what has gone, hunches, emotions, changeable loyalty

Ill Dignified or Reversed – A hankering after the past and that which is gone and never to return. Vanity and pride in past success and accomplishment creating a barrier to future success. A clinging to the past and outdated habits and customs. Exaggerated nostalgia.

The Six of Cups reversed is at best all about hankering over the past, which leaves a sadness that it is now gone. It is about remembering the good old days, but to such an extent that the memories impact quite strongly on the present – and not always in a positive way. This is a card about living in the past, and for the past, and not moving on with life. At its worst, this card is not just an over reflection on the past. Indeed, this card may even signify that past memories may not have been the most pleasant and you may feel that you can't move on because there is so much negativity and baggage still surrounding you. The Six of Cups, instead of containing happy memories, may contain some of the darker elements from the past. When these cups reverse, then in a figurative sense, their unpleasant-tasting poison spills out onto the floor for everyone to see. This may leave you feeling swamped by bad memories from the past as they swim around in the dark liquid squelching on the floor. However, this liquid that represents bad memories, if you like, can always be mopped up and squeezed back into the figurative cups. So the best course of action here is to stick some metaphorical "Clingfilm" over the cups to seal in that poison and bury them all deep in the garden. In other words, when this card reversed shows up, accept that the past should stay exactly there, in the past. Try to let go of any negative feelings and emotions from times gone by, so that these no longer hamper you in the future. And if it makes you feel better, go and dance on the grave of those cups and be happy that they have been planted firmly back where they belong.

- The past is past and long since gone, step back into the present, where you belong.

Hidden Meaning: The Six of Cups, together with the Two of Cups, may indicate a meeting with someone from the past. The Six of Cups together with The Lovers may indicate the end of a relationship.

VII Cups
The Lord of Illusionary Success

NUMERICAL VALUE	7
ELEMENT	Water
TETRAGRAMMATRON	Heh (Energy into Form)
LIFE ASPECT	Emotions
ASTROLOGICAL ASSOCIATIONS	Pisces, Cancer, Scorpio

Guideline Divinatory Meanings:

Keywords (Upright): New opportunities, choices, decisions, persistence in pursuing goals, inspiration through psychic experiences

Upright – A need to reflect upon choices. Sometimes too many choices and opportunities are presented, which need careful consideration if a grave error of judgement is to be avoided. May refer to a variety of choices of people; for example, marriage and other partners. The inquirer is faced with several choices; one of exceptional promise, but great perception is needed for this to be seen. This card may also indicate mystical experience of an inspiring kind.

The Seven of Cups is all about not letting things get out of control. You may find that situations are moving and changing fast and there will be a requirement for you to jump into the saddle and take charge of the reins. This could be a really good time for deciding what you would really like to achieve, and with this card in your spread, you may find that there will be a number of possibilities to choose from. Maybe now is a good time to reflect on your inner most thoughts and desires and take some time out to ensure that you make the right decisions. Some gain may be made by unselfish love.

- Lots of choices and decisions to make; the right one is there, for you to take.
- The "Illusion" card.

Keywords (Reversed): Opportunities to dispel illusions, sympathy for friends, indecision

Ill Dignified or Reversed – Reliance upon false hopes. Inaction causing the loss of opportunity. A fear of success. Self-delusion and indecision.

The Seven of Cups reversed is a complete opposite to its upright self. In its upright position, this card represents choice and the making of the right decisions. Imagine that each cup is full with a different choice or possibility. When these Seven Cups topple over as they turn upside down, all of those options subsequently trickle away. It is almost like all of the open doors have been closed and any hope of them opening up again is very misplaced. If the upright card is one of illusion, this is a card of self delusion. Not only are decisions possibly difficult at this time, it is actually questionable whether or not a choice even exists at all. When this card appears in the reversed position, then it could signify that you are feeling a little low and that you don't feel as if there is much you can do about a situation. Although things may seem bad, you can always wade through the mess on the floor made by the overturned cups. There is always a way forward, but the key here is in identifying it. Don't let things fool you into thinking all is lost and don't let good opportunities escape due to inaction.

- When all your choices are in the bin, pull them out and start again. When all possibilities are laid on the line, make a good choice; now's the time.

VIII Cups
The Lord of Abandoned Success

NUMERICAL VALUE	8
ELEMENT	Water
TETRAGRAMMATRON	Heh (Energy into Form)
LIFE ASPECT	Emotions
ASTROLOGICAL ASSOCIATIONS	Pisces, Cancer, Scorpio

Guideline Divinatory Meanings:

Keywords (Upright): Moves, personal power, leaving the past behind, dreams, self sacrifice, extravagance

Upright – A turning point, a severing of links with the past, which have become outdated. A turning away from established relationships and objects of affection, to facilitate progress to newer and deeper things. A change of perspective, a change of viewpoint. Security and attachment.

The Eight of Cups is symbolic of becoming somewhat bored with all that is familiar to you. With this card in your spread, you may feel that you have a dream that you really want to follow, but this in turn could mean leaving behind old friendships, partners, relationships, etc. Any decision of this magnitude will need all of your strength and courage, if this is what you feel is the right choice for you. This card suggests that you may have outgrown your current situation. The Eight of Cups may also indicate domestic changes and you may be feeling that now is the time to move on in your life. If you are already in a relationship, then it could mean you are searching for deeper commitment. However, all in all, when you are sure, and only when you are sure, as a summing up, this card implies that you may "live the dream!"

- When you're bored with all around you, it's time for off, to pastures new.
- A "Follow Your Dream" card. A card of women; and for women and female issues.

Keywords (Reversed): Caution in affectional matters, family responsibilities dominate, desertion of the well founded

Ill Dignified or Reversed – Abandonment of that which has been well founded in order to pursue an impossible ideal. Fantasy and risk. Restlessness and recklessness.

The Eight of Cups reversed is a relatively easy card to interpret. In its upright position it is all about personal empowerment and finding the courage to move onwards and upwards. There is a sense of needing to follow one's dreams no matter what. When this card reverses, however, all of those dreams come crashing onto the floor. There is a feeling that they have not only been given up on, the querent has positively walked away from them. The simple message here is not to rush into anything quickly, although you may be feeling somewhat restless at present, guard against being reckless. Stick with what you know and value right now. Most importantly don't give up on your dreams; scoop them all up off the floor, back into the metaphorical cups and strap them all to your back. Keep your dreams with you; don't walk away from them or indeed sacrifice them for an unworthy cause.

- When your dreams are on the floor, collect them up, and search for more.

IX Cups
The Lord of Material Happiness

NUMERICAL VALUE	9
ELEMENT	Water
TETRAGRAMMATRON	Heh (Energy into Form)
LIFE ASPECT	Emotions
ASTROLOGICAL ASSOCIATIONS	Pisces, Cancer, Scorpio

Guideline Divinatory Meanings:

Keywords (Upright): Happiness, dreams, reassessment of desires, wishes, hopes realized, emotional stability

Upright – An assured future, satisfaction, contentment, and physical well-being. Overcoming difficulty. Emotional stability, a benign outlook. Inner security which radiates a general aura of goodwill. Liberality, generosity of spirit, feelings of well-being.

CUPS

The Nine of Cups, sometimes referred to as "The Wish" card is possibly one of the best of all of the Minor Arcana cards. Nines are generally considered to be powerful cards and are linked to The Hermit card. Therefore, it could be described as a card of "seek and ye shall find." The Nine of Cups is also symbolic of a sense of fulfilment, joy, prosperity, abundance, and good feelings. On an emotional level, relationships are good and creativity high. Fortune is also starred for: personal finances, personal goals, and general harmony and well-being. With this card in your spread, now is the time to make a wish, and who knows, it may just come true.

- Follow your dream, whatever it may be; wishes can come true, you will see.
- A "Wish card."

Keywords (Reversed): Overspending, caution against loss of credit cards, money-related issues, errors, vanity, hospitality abuse, vicissitudes

Ill Dignified or Reversed – Falling into error, complacency, vanity, and self indulgence. Sometimes, shortage of money due to spendthrift tendencies or loss of credit cards. Sentimentality and an overlooking of the faults in others, which can lead to abuse of hospitality.

The Nine of Cups reversed is not a "Wish card" as it is in an upright position. If anything, this card reversed, is more about wishes not coming true. Nines usually signify a certain amount of completion where situations are assessed to establish their success or lack of it. But this card reversed is more symbolic of lack of completion and wishes not being fulfilled. There may be money worries. Indeed, now may not be a good time to embark on a gambling spree. There is also a sense of vanity, complacency, and over confidence with this card, which in turn may lead to an abuse of the hospitality of others. A simple way to think of this reversed card is that once the cups spill out their wishes, there's none left to be granted. The advice here is to chase those wishes, run after them, because until you catch up with them, they can't be made to come true.

- Even if your dream didn't come true, there's still nice things, on the cards for you.

X Cups
The Lord of Perfected Success

NUMERICAL VALUE	10
ELEMENT	Water
TETRAGRAMMATRON	Heh (Energy into Form)
LIFE ASPECT	Emotions
ASTROLOGICAL ASSOCIATIONS	Pisces, Cancer, Scorpio

Guideline Divinatory Meanings:

Keywords (Upright): Family, friendships, relationships, completion, security

Upright – Lasting happiness and security, although sometimes this may be indicative of being in a rut. Good reputation and honor, true friendship, and happy family life. Perfect love and concord between people. A search for fulfilment is marked with success. A peaceful and secure environment.

The Ten of Cups, as with all of the Tens of the Minor Arcana, is symbolic of the end of a suit and the final good or bad of that element. Luckily, the Ten of Cups is a card for good. Generally, this card indicates stable happy families, friends, and relationships. In the sense of the family, then this is a card of feelings of permanent security, where the whole family is committed to family values and working together towards a greater good. In the sense of friendship, joy and contentment are starred. For existing relationships, you may feel emotionally satisfied. With this card in your spread, it suggests that family, friends, and relationships are playing an important role in your life, and you are building up a secure network of caring and trustworthy people around you that will support you into the future.

- All the pain has led to gain, and now joy and happiness can commence their reign.
- A "Wish" card.

Keywords (Reversed): Avoid emotional crossfire, reversal of feeling, inconstant emotions, loss of friendship, family issues

Ill Dignified or Reversed – The manipulation of society for personal gain. Loss of friendship. Family quarrels. Sudden violent disruption of an ordered environment and ordered routine. Anti-social actions. Look for signs of new adolescents or new births.

The Ten of Cups reversed is like its upright self, related to a family environment. However, unlike the Ten of Cups upright, this card is about tension within a family. It suggests that what was once a happy, stable, and loving family environment is being threatened by some form of discord and tension caused by an individual within it. This is not a card that indicates a total breakdown of a happy family; it represents more someone within that circle who is being a bit of a nuisance and causing a degree of friction. Within a group of friends, this also holds true. Imagine when the Ten of Cups reverses; all of the cups except one land upside down. The ones on the floor come safely to rest, but one stands out among them, sticking its figurative head above the parapet, if you like. When this card appears reversed in a spread, now may not be the time to make waves. Watch out for people who are trying to dictate to you; an aggressive stance may not necessarily be the best way forward. This card reversed can also indicate that someone within a family or friendship environment may need some help at present and this could be a reason why they may be behaving oddly or causing problems. Either way, the figurative cup just needs a bit of a shove, in order to get it lined up in the same position as the others. Then balance and harmony can be restored.

- When in the ointment lands a fly, hang any troublemaker out to dry.

Page Cups
The Princess of the Waters
The Lotus of the Palace of the Floods

NUMERICAL VALUE	7
ELEMENT	Water
ELEMENTAL NAME	Earth of Water
TETRAGRAMMATRON	Heh (Energy into Form)
HAIR COLOR	Brown
EYE COLOR	Blue or Brown
LIFE ASPECT	Emotions
ASTROLOGICAL ASSOCIATIONS	Pisces, Cancer, Scorpio

Guideline Divinatory Meanings:

Keywords (Upright): News, new projects, higher education, or learning

Upright – A symbol of imagination. May indicate a time for quiet reflection. Depending upon surrounding cards: a messenger bringing news of an engagement, marriage or birth. A reflective, poetic, quiet, and artistic person, gentle and kind. A person with a wealth of knowledge, giving freely his advice. A person gifted with much foresight.

The Page of Cups, when related to a person, would symbolize a male or female under the age of 22 years; indeed, it could even be a child. Normally, Pages represent the bringing forth or delivery of news, and in the case of the Page of Cups, this could mean messages about family, romance, or even love. This card is also symbolic of beneficial messages, a business partnership or maybe even a new relationship, that in turn may lead to emotional harmony. Marriage proposals, engagements, and new projects and business enterprises are often associated with this card and any reunions with a friend or partner are well starred. This is a nice card to have in your spread and it suggests that there could be some interesting news coming your way.

- Hair of brown, eyes brown or blue, a kind person, has wonderful news for you.

Keywords (Reversed): Uncovered deception, failure to commit, gossip

Ill Dignified or Reversed – Depending upon surrounding cards: A deception will be uncovered. A failure to make meaningful commitments and shallow self indulgence. A person with much surface and shallow knowledge, a "jack of all trades." A scheming person that is selfish and keeps his knowledge to himself. He has an appreciation of the beautiful, but is not applied enough to become an artist. A person who is lazy and given to lies and harmful gossip.

The Page of Cups reversed is not such a likeable character as his upright self. Instead of being a reflective, poetic, kind, and gentle soul, this card reversed represents someone who is much different. When he turns upside down, the Page has become completely floored and is far too lazy to pick himself/herself up. The fine wine in his/her cup has spilled on the floor and he/she is quite bitter about its loss. The Page reversed may be described as someone who is shallow, selfish, secretive and somewhat lazy. He no longer has a cup brimming over with metaphorical happy letters, messages, and correspondence. His cup is now empty. For this reason, anything he has to bring may be tainted. Therefore, when he shows up in a spread, don't expect him to deliver nice letters or happy news. If you are in a relationship, then the only type of message he/she would bring would be a "Dear John" letter. When this Page is reversed and too lazy to get up, the best thing to do is walk quickly away before he catches up with you.

- Eyes brown or blue and hair of brown, his letters, may make you feel down.

Knight Cups
The Lord of the Waves and the Waters
The King of the Hosts of the Sea

NUMERICAL VALUE	4
ELEMENT	Water
ELEMENTAL NAME	Fire of Water
TETRAGRAMMATRON	Heh (Energy into Form)
HAIR COLOR	Brown
EYE COLOR	Gray or Blue
LIFE ASPECT	Emotions
ASTROLOGICAL ASSOCIATIONS	Pisces, Cancer, Scorpio

Guideline Divinatory Meanings:

Keywords (Upright): Travel to water, strong emotions, optimism, romance, invitations, excitement, thoughts of love and affection

Upright – Change and new excitements, particularly of a romantic nature. Invitations, opportunities, and offers. A person who is a bringer of ideas, opportunity, and offers. He is constantly bored and in constant need of stimulation, but also artistic and refined. A person who is amiable, intelligent, full of high principals, but a dreamer who can be easily led or discouraged.

The Knight of Cups, as a person, is symbolic of someone who is very much a Romeo teen type who spends hours in his room. He could be described as both romantic and emotional. Indeed, this person is just the sort of person who would be very upset if their pet rabbit died and he also has a tendency to be a little on the moody side. However, he is fiercely loyal to those he loves and is generally very enthusiastic. In terms of what this card could symbolize, it is often associated with travel to water, whether it is a lake, stream, or sea. A boat trip of some kind may also be involved. Romance could be in the air and you may find yourself faced with an invitation on which to ponder. In terms of a relationship, this card is indicative of a caring and sensitive man who desires a relationship that is not shallow and has some depth to it. This is a card of strong emotions, optimism, and excitement.

- Hair color brown, eyes blue or gray, he's a likeable romantic, who's in your way.

Keywords (Reversed): Unreliability, false promises, opposition to true affectional desires

Ill Dignified or Reversed – Unreliability and recklessness. Depending on surrounding cards: fraud, embezzlement, false promises, and trickery. A person who is a congenital liar, someone who has trouble discerning the end of the truth and the beginning of falsehood.

The Knight of Cups reversed, just like his younger counterpart the Page of Cups reversed, is not such a likeable character. Some of his key personality traits include unreliability, recklessness, and sometimes he can even be a downright liar. Deception is a major theme when this card reversed shows up. When he turns upside down, his falling horse lands on top of him and squeezes out his positive traits. Any positivity in his cup has flowed away. This Knight reversed is someone who is gloomy, depressed, and fickle. One message that he does bring though is a warning to beware if you are planning any boat trips or journeys by sea. Before setting off, make sure that all of your safety equipment is checked. In a metaphorical sense, when this reversed card turns up in your spread, help him back onto his horse but ensure you send him packing with a swift slap on his steed's back.

- Hair color brown, eyes blue or gray, this is a reckless character, getting in your way.

Queen Cups
Queen of the Thrones of the Waters

NUMERICAL VALUE	4
ELEMENT	Water
ELEMENTAL NAME	Water of Water
TETRAGRAMMATRON	Heh (Energy into Form)
HAIR COLOR	Golden Brown
EYE COLOR	Blue
LIFE ASPECT	Emotions
ASTROLOGICAL ASSOCIATIONS	Pisces, Cancer, Scorpio

Guideline Divinatory Meanings:

Keywords (Upright): Trust, goodness, intelligence, wisdom honesty

Upright – A happy card that indicates balance and harmony; also symbolizes high achievements made possible by the use of imagination. A woman who is highly imaginative and artistically gifted, affectionate, and romantic in outlook, and creates an otherworldly atmosphere around herself. A woman who lacks common sense, but is highly intuitive and sometimes psychic and dreamy. Atmospheres, other people, and events can easily influence her.

The Queen of Cups, when symbolic of a person, is someone who is virtuous and honest. With this card in your spread, someone who is wise, intelligent, intuitive, and honest may be coming into your life at some point in the near future. She will possibly be a mature person with a creative nature and someone who gives advice based upon intuition and experience. In general, Queens are the cards that indicate a time for growth and development. Therefore, the nurturing of psychic powers, romances, and family in general are all well starred. For those already in a relationship, the Queen puts an emphasis upon stability. It is a card of strong relations and domestic happiness. You may even receive an offer of friendship or a greater or deeper level of commitment from an existing one. This card is a happy card and a very positive one to have in your spread.

- Hair golden brown and eye color blue, this is a lady, with affection for you.

Keywords (Reversed): Unreliability, undependable woman, fecklessness

Ill Dignified or Reversed – Fecklessness. A woman who cannot be trusted, someone who is a dreamer, unreliable, and cannot be depended upon. She is swift to change her opinions without reason or good cause. A woman who can sometimes be hysterical. She may even lead others down the wrong path in pursuit of some idle fantasy.

The Queen of Cups reversed is a lady who uses emotions to serve her own ends. Instead of being a trustworthy kind of person, this lady is much less helpful. She comes across as quite an emotionally dark character. Internally, she may have a number of conflicts going on in her head. At its very worst, this is a card of someone who is mentally disturbed, possibly very depressed, prone to extreme mood swings and/or may be suffering from some kind of hormonal imbalance. When the Queen of Cups turns upside down, it is like she falls to the floor and begins to drown all of the emotions that have spilled out of her cup onto the floor. This is a lady in need of some symbolic mouth-to-mouth resuscitation. When she arrives in a spread, the best course of action is to help her back onto her throne and ensure she is alright. However, you are at your peril, if you let her "get into your head," as you don't want to end up as mixed up as she is.

- Hair golden brown and eye color blue, her topsy-turvy world, is waiting for you.

King Cups
The Prince of the Chariot of the Waters

NUMERICAL VALUE	4
ELEMENT	Water
ELEMENTAL NAME	Air of Water
TETRAGRAMMATRON	Heh (Energy into Form)
HAIR COLOR	Fair
EYE COLOR	Blue
LIFE ASPECT	Emotions
ASTROLOGICAL ASSOCIATIONS	Pisces, Cancer, Scorpio

Guideline Divinatory Meanings:

Keywords (Upright): Respect, family, artistic tendencies, mature love

Upright – A person who commands respect, but not love. A man of business or law, considerate and responsible. He is kind, but ambitious, and a skilled negotiator. He is a born manipulator, someone who has arrived in a position of power by the use of the brain, as opposed to brawn. He avoids taking people into his confidence and often works in secret or behind the scenes. He is a seeker of power, with hidden motives, often distrusted or feared by those around him.

The King of Cups, as with all Kings, symbolizes the taking forward of everything to the next level. Whereas Queens typically help to solidify a situation, the King helps to, metaphorically speaking, break free of the castle walls to push everything just that little bit further. As a person, this card is representative of someone who finds creative success in the more arty disciplines. He may also be skilled in the fields of drama, writing, music, or architecture. Other professions include: historian, chef, bookshop owner, museum curator, restorer, painter, and decorator. This card has been likened to a kind version of the "Godfather" and his realm likened to his family over whom he is fiercely protective. As a father figure, he is very protective towards his family and would seek retribution if anyone deliberately hurt any of his relations. He is also the type of person to "bail out" those he loves. Indeed, the King of Cups, as a person, is a reliable, well-meaning individual who takes a disciplined approach to life. In general, this card can indicate new starts as well and is also linked to love. You may find that with this card in your spread, you are building up the courage to approach someone romantically. Or it could be that you wish to become a better provider for your family. Artistic interests are also well starred with this card.

- Hair color fair and with eyes of blue this is someone kind, to watch over you.

Keywords (Reversed): Lack of moral sense, gossip, may indicate an unscrupulous man

Ill Dignified or Reversed – A violent, unscrupulous, dishonest man who is likely to be involved in double dealing. His only responsibilities are to himself and he has no moral sense. He may try to involve his associates in scandal and generally undesirable activity, as he himself may be drawn. Take great care in personal or business affairs.

The King of Cups reversed, although a more emotionally balanced person still has issues and negative traits of his own. Just like the Knight reversed, this King reversed is also prone to dishonesty. However, he has much more authority to add to any deceptions, making him quite a negatively formidable character. He is someone to be avoided at all costs. His cup is full of symbolic poison, but he fills himself up on it, before it has a chance to escape when he tumbles upside down. He is both ruthless and unscrupulous and lacking any sense of morals. If you see this King upside down with his throne on top, take the opportunity to run away as fast as you can.

- Hair color fair and eyes of blue, try keeping this man, away from you.

Ace Swords
The Root of the Powers of Air

NUMERICAL VALUE	5
SEASON	Autumn
DIRECTION	East
ELEMENT	Air
TETRAGRAMMATRON	Vau (Stabilization of Form)
LIFE ASPECT	Intellectual Activity
ASTROLOGICAL ASSOCIATIONS	Gemini, Libra, Aquarius

Guideline Divinatory Meanings:

Keywords (Upright): Clarity of thought, new beginnings, new challenges

Upright – Total and complete change of mind. In its purest form, the Ace is symbolic of strongly constituted authority, and pursuit of ultimate truth. Triumph, victory and success, a rebirth and a new beginning.

The Ace of Swords is all about clarity of mind and clear-cut thought. It is a card about new beginnings and possibly new ventures. There may well be a good opportunity to achieve success. Any rewards, however, will come through clear, well-reasoned thinking and careful consideration of any decisions that may have to be made. At this time, it is possible that you have a clearer idea of what you want out of any relationships, and you may find that you are working passionately towards your goals.

- With clarity of thought in mind and deed, a new start is all you need.

Keywords (Reversed): Division of ideas, faulty analysis, mental blocks, suppression of news

Ill Dignified or Reversed – Confusion, exaggeration in thought, aggression, force, destruction, and the misuse of power. Possibly death in the sense of a venture, but this depends upon other cards.

The Ace of Swords reversed is about false starts and mental blocks. When this card is turned upside down, the once-keen edges of the sword's blade are dulled as it becomes embedded in the ground. This could mean that there is currently a lack of mental clarity, as the querent's senses may generally not be as sharp as usual. This card also symbolizes the misuse or mishandling of power and some legal problems. When the Ace of Swords shows up reversed in a spread, there is a sense that it is a negative force and it warns about placing restrictions on people by fear instead of reason. There may also be the death of an intellectual venture as the creative spark normally associated with an upright Ace, has fizzled out in its reversed state. The advice here is to leave that figurative sword planted in the ground as its blade is already dull and of little use. However, if you water it, who knows, it may yet sprout forth green shoots. In other words, sometimes, in order to move forward, watching, waiting, and taking a view on a situation may be the best way to proceed.

- A promising venture about to fail may find its success lies lost in the mail.

II Swords
The Lord of Peace Restored

NUMERICAL VALUE	2
ELEMENT	Air
TETRAGRAMMATRON	Vau (Stabilization of Form)
LIFE ASPECT	Intellectual Activity
ASTROLOGICAL ASSOCIATIONS	Gemini, Libra, Aquarius

Guideline Divinatory Meanings:

Keywords (Upright): Decisions, choice, harmony, balance, opposing factions, strength, obstacles overcome by love

Upright – Courage, delicate, and precarious balance in adversity. Differences resolved, relief, restoration of peace, truce, a weight off the mind.

The Two of Swords normally shows two swords being crossed. Some decks depict the Two of Swords with a person blindfolded holding two crossed swords, but the emphasis is on the fact that the swords are crossed. They represent two opposing ideas and possibly a need to either choose the best route from the ideas or balance two opposing factions. With this card in your spread, it is possible that you may find yourself faced with a choice consisting of two alternatives, and by making the correct decision, rifts could be healed or issues resolved. Impartiality is a good word to observe when the Two of Swords appears, particularly if you are in the middle of a family row. This is a card of moving towards balance and harmony.

- When you don't know what to do, try to get the balance right, that's the clue.

Keywords (Reversed): Duplicity, trouble with possessions, social disappointments

Ill Dignified or Reversed – Disloyalty, aggression, willful misguidance and misleading advice, dishonesty, "jiggery-pokery," and misrepresentation.

The Two of Swords reversed is a card of conflict and an inability to achieve balance. In its upright position, the Two of Swords is all about balancing opposing factions. When this card reversed shows up, it is more likely that any opposing factions will begin to fight, let alone strive to resolve any differences. There is certainly a sense of disunity and disharmony with this card reversed. When it turns upside down, the neat crossing of the two swords in the upright position is lost, and they lie in disarray on the floor. There is now no room for conformity or unity here. Decision making may become difficult and there is also a warning to watch out for any dishonest dealings, as some people may not be as trustworthy as they may seem. Any marital issues must be handled with care. The reversed swords must be brought back into balance, so they need to be picked up separated and planted firmly away from one another in the ground. Once a solid base is achieved this will allow you time to work out the best course of action. Weigh up all situations and people carefully and ensure that any polar opposites or people with conflicting ideas are kept apart, for the time being at least.

- When feelings are low and blue, make the right choices; it's up to you.

Hidden Meaning: The Two of Swords and the Ten of Coins may signify money because of a divorce settlement.

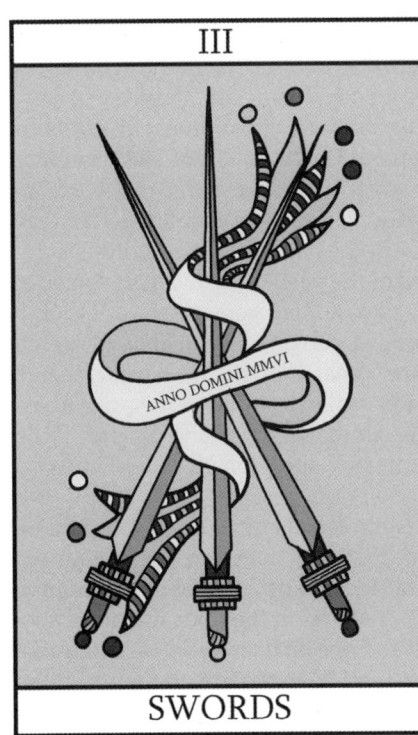

III Swords
The Lord of Sorrow

NUMERICAL VALUE	3
ELEMENT	Air
TETRAGRAMMATRON	Vau (Stabilization of Form)
LIFE ASPECT	Intellectual Activity
ASTROLOGICAL ASSOCIATIONS	Gemini, Libra, Aquarius

Guideline Divinatory Meanings:

Keywords (Upright): Growth, heavy responsibilities, business issues, legal issues, antagonism

Upright – Sorrow and extreme pain, but all with a positive view in end: upheaval, separation, disruption, and discord. Heartbreak, tears, strife, conflict. The clearing of that which is obsolete to make way for that to come. Establishment of something better.

The Three of Swords is a card which has an aura of sadness about it and can be indicative of unhappy moments. It can also symbolize a love triangle and possible relationship issues. This is not one of the best cards in the deck by far to have in a spread, but what you need to realize is that although it is not the easiest of times right now, do not lose sight of the end, as this is much more positive. Although you may feel like bottling everything up right now, the truth will eventually "out" and this all will be to a positive end.

- With heavy heart full of sorrow, don't despair, there's always tomorrow. With a broken heart full of despair, there's still love around, to aid it's repair.
- The "Misery" card.

Keywords (Reversed): Friendship issues, social splits, idealism

Ill Dignified or Reversed – Spiritual and mental confusion, loss, discord, dishonesty, and upset. War, breaking of a truce, quarrels, and enmity. Physical or mental issues.

The Three of Swords reversed, just like the Two of Swords reversed, contains an element of disunity and disharmony. If you liken two of the three swords to a girlfriend and boyfriend out on their first date, the third sword would represent the "gooseberry" who tags along. Both parties like "the gooseberry," just not when they want to spend time with each other. This of course could lead to quarrels and arguments which are also symbolic of the Three of Swords reversed. Upside down, two swords fall together leaving the third out in the cold. This can represent a situation where all of the parties involved are forced together, but only two of them genuinely want to be together and the third person is somewhat a "spare wheel," if you like. What is worse, perhaps, is that the other two parties make no secret of their negative feelings about the third person being around. This makes for an unhappy situation all round. When this card is in its reversed position, the negative aspects of the Three of Swords upright are also felt. What this means is that any hurt and upset may run much deeper and last much longer. Turned on its head, all of the Swords on the floor that now lie in a two together and one on its own arrangement, need to be picked up and have their metaphorical hilts banged together. The best way forward is to come to some kind of mutually beneficial truce.

- Feeling left out in the cold, dive back in, be really bold.

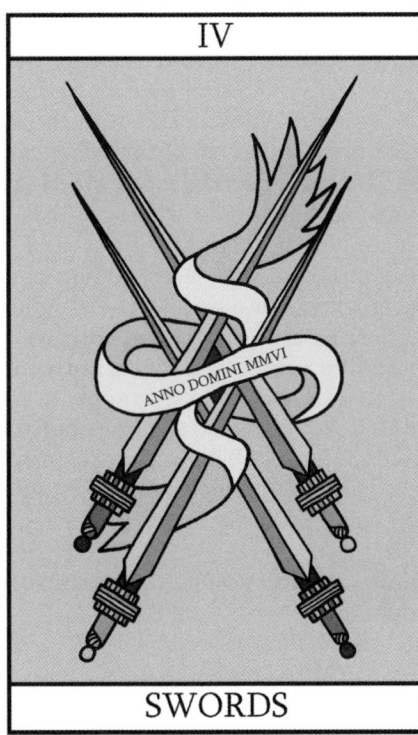

IV Swords
The Lord of Rest from Strife

NUMERICAL VALUE	4
ELEMENT	Air
TETRAGRAMMATRON	Vau (Stabilization of Form)
LIFE ASPECT	Intellectual Activity
ASTROLOGICAL ASSOCIATIONS	Gemini, Libra, Aquarius

Guideline Divinatory Meanings:

Keywords (Upright): Consolidation, meditation, peace, calm, recovery, rewarded patience

Upright – Retreat, withdrawal, peace established through arms. Rest, recovery, medical care, recuperation from battle and relief from anxiety or sorrow.

The Four of Swords is sometimes referred to as a card of meditation because it is symbolic of a period of calm after a storm. Now could be a time for you to get away from it all and reflect upon everything that has happened; especially concentrate on things that may not have been so positive in your life. You may find that now is a good time to re-energize yourself after a period of turmoil. If you have been facing a long period of physical/emotional stress, disagreements, misunderstandings, verbal abuse, and general disharmony, then this card indicates that a period of rest and recuperation is needed, particularly if you have been feeling under the weather or unwell. A quiet stable scene is what is needed here, as this is a card for building up your physical and mental health.

- After the storm, you need calm and rest; put your feet up – that's what's best.
- The "Rest and Recuperation" card.

Keywords (Reversed): Give and take, determination

Ill Dignified or Reversed – Banishment, enforced isolation, seclusion, confinement, cowardice, low mood, and failure of nerve.

The Four of Swords reversed is a card symbolic of seclusion. As the Four of Swords turns upside down, the swords stick neatly into the ground forming a line or shield behind which the querent can hide. This card reversed is one of self imposed restrictions, seclusion and isolation. It is almost as if you are hiding behind the figurative swords that have stuck in the earth. When this card reversed appears, it is a time to guard against any negative feelings and emotions as you do not want to become depressed. Artistic ventures are not particularly well starred at the moment. In order to move forward, you need to come out from your figurative hiding place behind your swords. Tackle any obstacles in your way, and if at first you don't succeed, then try and try again.

- Feeling low and secluded, get some rest, or be deluded.

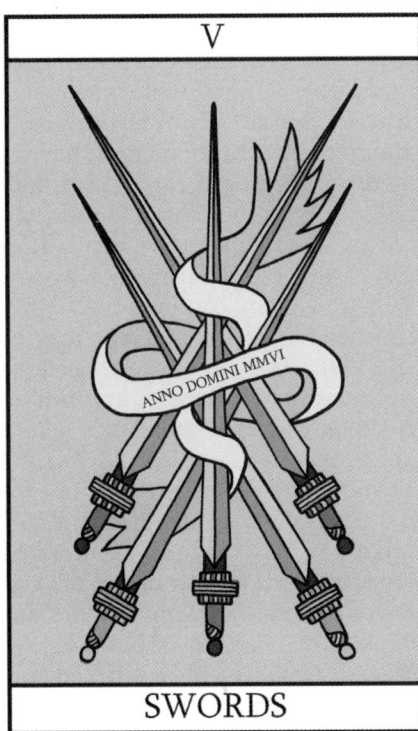

V Swords
The Lord of Defeat

NUMERICAL VALUE	5
ELEMENT	Air
TETRAGRAMMATRON	Vau (Stabilization of Form)
LIFE ASPECT	Intellectual Activity
ASTROLOGICAL ASSOCIATIONS	Gemini, Libra, Aquarius

Guideline Divinatory Meanings:

Keywords (Upright): Change, tension, frustration, arguments

Upright – Defeat, loss, non-accomplishment, low self esteem, a need to curb futile belligerence, accept the inevitable, and swallow pride. Negative thoughts and attitudes.

The Five of Swords indicates a period in your life that must be managed carefully to achieve the best possible outcome. It is often difficult to remain objective, particularly when having lost an argument the victor has a habit of gloating. However, with this card in your spread, that is exactly what you should do. Arguments that may be a bit difficult to win shouldn't be fought, as it may prove better to walk away and learn from your experiences. This card also indicates that you should only take on board as much responsibility as you are both comfortable with and can cope with. The Five of Swords symbolizes tension, anxiety, and frustrations that lead to arguments, so compromise and the ability to listen are the keywords here.

- The cunning fox who runs away, lives to hunt another day. Time to concede and walk away, you know it's painful, but better that way.
- The "Losing a Fight" card and a "Bully" card.

Keywords (Reversed): Great effort, faith breaks the barrier

Ill Dignified or Reversed – Paranoia, indecision, malice, spite, or someone acting as such in personal affairs.

The Five of Swords reversed is about malice and spite. It may even suggest that someone is acting in this way in your affairs. When this card turns upside down the swords or daggers have become drawn and point straight at you. It is almost as though a fight is in the offing. However, unlike the Seven of Swords, upright, this battle is not necessarily lost. There is a suggestion that you may still be able to win any conflicts, but your victory may be somewhat hollow. Or this may even be a struggle that drags on and on, particularly if your opponent is behaving in an underhanded manner. When this card shows up, take note of any suspicions you may have. In this instance, it may be more beneficial to walk away from the figurative daggers. With daggers drawn, this is a battle that you probably can't win outright, or your victory may be a hollow one. Walk away and preserve your strength to fight another day.

- When you're faced with malice and spite, turn the other cheek; you know that's right.

VI Swords

The Lord of Earned Success

NUMERICAL VALUE	6
ELEMENT	Air
TETRAGRAMMATRON	Vau (Stabilization of Form)
LIFE ASPECT	Intellectual Activity
ASTROLOGICAL ASSOCIATIONS	Gemini, Libra, Aquarius

Guideline Divinatory Meanings:

Keywords (Upright): Dissipation, mastership, stability, a firm stance, steady progress

Upright – Gradual change, movement or travel away from difficulty or imminent danger. The solution of current problems. Long journeys and passage from pain. Obstacles that are overcome.

The Six of Swords is a card that symbolizes balance and harmony after a period of turmoil. It is symbolic of the restoration of equilibrium to a situation. It is a slow but sure, steady progress after a period of turbulence. It is an indication that difficulties and challenges have been overcome and anxieties quashed. However, there is more to this card, because as well as indicating progression away from difficulties, it is also symbolic of answers to puzzles. If you have a brain teaser to solve or a mathematical question that is posing a problem, then this card indicates that the answer may just lie round the corner. With this card in your spread, the attributes of peace, equilibrium, harmony, and the solutions to problems are well starred.

- Take a passage away from pain; this way you'll have more to gain.

Keywords (Reversed): Delayed affectional matters, great effort can bring progress, temporary relief

Ill Dignified or Reversed – Developments that are unexpected, temporary relief from difficulties, need for continuing effort and strength. Once one obstacle is surmounted, another presents itself.

The Six of Swords reversed is a card about perseverance and not giving up, because just as you think you have overcome one obstacle, another one pops up to get in the way. When these six swords fall down as they reverse, they fall into a muddy lake. It is like everything is lost, particularly as the water is too cloudy to see anything in it. When this card reversed shows up, it can be symbolic of a refusal to get to the heart of a matter. Any half-hearted attempts at resolving anything will only result in patching up the problem and any relief will be temporary. The only way to resolve anything here is to tackle it head on. In this situation, you need to put on your full diving equipment and get your hands dirty while dragging along the lake's bottom to find all of those lost swords. Continued effort is essential here; giving up before the end is in sight is not really an option.

- When the end is in sight, don't give in, hold your nerve and then you'll win.

VII Swords
The Lord of Unstable Effort

NUMERICAL VALUE	7
ELEMENT	Air
TETRAGRAMMATRON	Vau (Stabilization of Form)
LIFE ASPECT	Intellectual Activity
ASTROLOGICAL ASSOCIATIONS	Gemini, Libra, Aquarius

Guideline Divinatory Meanings:

Keywords (Upright): Cunning, stealth, caution in the face of adversity, guard against theft

Upright – Sudden desire and impulse. A card of caution in the face of opposition. Change of residence, job or possibly both. An indication of triumph in the face of adversity, but must be through cunning. No real progress, through lack of purpose.

The Seven of Swords is sometimes called the "Thief" card as traditional symbolism shows someone quickly managing to steal away with five of the seven swords. This card is indicative of someone trying to steal something from you. It does not necessarily need to be a physical thing. Indeed, it could be something else like your reputation, honor, time, ideas, or good standing. However, in order to deal with the situation, cunning and stealth must be used. A head-on confrontation may result in the theft being simply denied and the perpetrator avoiding detection or getting away unchallenged. Should you find yourself in such a situation, then the advice here is: Think like a thief to catch a thief, and use all of your shrewdness. A different approach will help to obtain much better results for you. But always bear in mind that you need to be wary of hidden motives.

- Defeat a thief by using stealth, otherwise he'll steal your wealth.
- The" Thief" card.

Keywords (Reversed): Positive thinking, convert weakness to strength, faith fights discord

Ill Dignified or Reversed – Counsel and specific advice. Reluctance to carry through daring actions when necessary. Failure of nerve and indecision. Surrender when victory is almost in sight. Inability and reluctance to complete what has been started.

The Seven of Swords reversed is about the reluctance or failure to carry through daring actions when necessary. It is also a card of giving up when the end is nearly in sight. However, the Seven of Swords in its upright position has a traditional meaning of being a "Thief card," whereby someone is trying to steal something from you – whether it is your reputation or something more material like your wallet. For this reason, the Seven of Swords reversed also has a thief element attached to it. As the Seven of Swords reverses or turns upside down, the thief in this scenario loses all of his swords on the floor. Although he has stolen something, in this instance it has done him/her no good whatsoever. For this reason this card reversed carries two warnings, do not give up and do not use dubious tactics when trying to reach your goal. Simply pick up all of your figurative swords; nothing underhanded or fancy is required, just plain simple hard work.

- With a cunning grin and heart full of malice, the only thing stolen, is a poisoned chalice.

VIII Swords
The Lord of Shortened Force

NUMERICAL VALUE	8
ELEMENT	Air
TETRAGRAMMATRON	Vau (Stabilization of Form)
LIFE ASPECT	Intellectual Activity
ASTROLOGICAL ASSOCIATIONS	Gemini, Libra, Aquarius

Guideline Divinatory Meanings:

Keywords (Upright): Personal power, focus, feeling trapped, lessons to be learned

Upright – Jealousy, often from colleagues or family, crisis and enforced isolation, health-related issues and oppressiveness, major obstacles and difficult circumstances dictated by fate.

The Eight of Swords is a card of restriction and feelings of being trapped by circumstances. It is possible that you may find yourself in a catch twenty-two situation where you almost feel as if you are "damned if you do" and "damned if you don't." The Eight of Swords is also indicative of people who may be envious of you and it symbolizes self imposed restrictions and isolation. Should this be the case, then the advice here is to not lose hope because progress in your situation can be achieved. Just because you may think that you are not going to achieve your desired outcome, does not necessarily mean that you won't. This is a card of being aware of your circumstances and keeping the faith. Once you have managed to free yourself from any restrictions or negative circumstances you will feel a renewed sense of purpose.

- Discard the ties and walk free, remove the blindfold, and then you'll see.
- The "Trapped" card.

Keywords (Reversed): Experience, problems left behind

Ill Dignified or Reversed – Hard work reaping little reward, frustration, upset, low mood. Effort being exercised in the wrong place. Change and liberation. Moving away from a problem rather than finding the solution.

The Eight of Swords reversed is like its upright counterpart, all about being trapped within a set of circumstances. However, with this card reversed, there is also a sense of isolation. When this card turns upside down, all of the eight swords, forming a figurative barrier in front of the querent, have now fallen to the floor in a heap. The immediate obstruction has been removed but there is still a pile of sharp swords on the floor to scramble across. This suggests that there still needs to be some pain to achieve the gain, but maybe you don't want to go through it. Or maybe you feel that the whole situation is just too intense. For this reason you may feel trapped in a no-win situation. The only way to win when this card shows up in your spread is to accept that moving away from any problems will not solve them. The swords have fallen away hence the main barriers to any solutions have gone. But you still need to walk over those sharp blades to reach your goal. Don't give up, put on your strongest walking shoes with the thickest heels and trample all over the swords. There is always a way to free yourself without getting hurt, but the key is to figure out the best way to do it.

- Get rid of the chains and set yourself free; this really is, the best way to be.

IX Swords
The Lord of Despair and Cruelty

NUMERICAL VALUE	9
ELEMENT	Air
TETRAGRAMMATRON	Vau (Stabilization of Form)
LIFE ASPECT	Intellectual Activity
ASTROLOGICAL ASSOCIATIONS	Gemini, Libra, Aquarius

Guideline Divinatory Meanings:

Keywords (Upright): Contemplation, reassessment, dreams, wisdom

Upright – Deception, premonitions and bad dreams, suffering and depression, cruelty, disappointment, violence, loss, and scandal. All of these may be overcome through faith and calculated inaction. This is the card of the martyr, and with it, comes new life out of suffering.

The Nine of Swords, like all nines, is a card of contemplation and reassessment. Often, nines are associated with obtaining what you desire, but sometimes having too much of what you desire, or endless possibilities can pose a problem in itself. This card suggests that you may have quite a lot on your mind at the moment. You may be looking for solutions to problems and it feels as if all of the answers are swirling around in your head. This, in turn, may cause some sleeping difficulties as you may be feeling generally anxious. However, this card also brings with it a sense that things are becoming blown out of proportion and that the solution may be much less complex. The message is clear, although you may feel like you are in a bad dream; simply wake up and see it for what it is: only a bad dream. All of the answers are there and you just need to listen to your inner voice.

- Sometimes things aren't as they seem; you will wake up from this bad dream.
- The "Nightmare" card.

Keywords (Reversed): Renunciation, caution, fixed attitudes

Ill Dignified or Reversed – Distrust and suspicion, despair, misery, and spite. Total isolation away from comfort and help. Sometimes depending upon surrounding cards: institutionalization, self-destructive behavior, confinement, and non-engagement.

The Nine of Swords reversed is a very similar card to its upright self and symbolizes insomnia due to problems causing sleepless nights. When this card turns upside down, each of the nine swords clatters one by one slowly to the ground. With all of this constant noise, you might find that it's very difficult to sleep right now. Indeed, the Nine of Swords is sometimes referred to as the "Nightmare" card. With all of those metaphorical swords falling to the floor, there's so much noise going on around you, that you probably can't even get to sleep! In other words, when this card shows up reversed in your spread, you feel that things are really weighing down on your mind. You may be feeling so miserable at the moment that life just doesn't feel like fun right now. The advice here is to try to guard against mistrust and believe that wisdom and love will always win out in the end. Total isolation right now may not be good for you. You need to realize that your woes or the metaphorical swords that fell on the floor are only there temporarily. You need to hang them all back on the wall where they belong and hammer them in with strong nails to ensure that they don't become problematic again. When you confront your fears and secure those fallen swords, you will then have the peace and quiet to fall asleep and have some well deserved sleep and sweet dreams.

- Sleepless nights are on the wane; soon you'll feel yourself again.

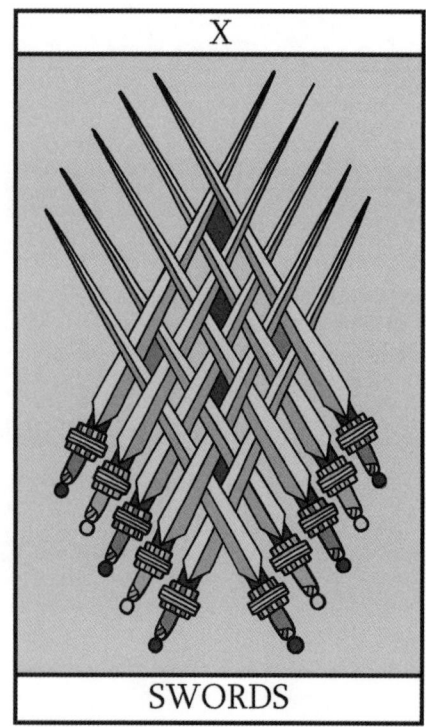

X Swords
The Lord of Ruin

NUMERICAL VALUE	10
ELEMENT	Air
TETRAGRAMMATRON	Vau (Stabilization of Form)
LIFE ASPECT	Intellectual Activity
ASTROLOGICAL ASSOCIATIONS	Gemini, Libra, Aquarius

Guideline Divinatory Meanings:

Keywords (Upright): Conclusions, end points, completion

Upright – Ruin, desolation, disruption, although generally, this refers to a group rather than an individual. Unhappiness, sudden tough luck, mishaps, muggings, or personal robbery. There is cause for optimism; as the lowest point in the cycle, from now on things can only get better, the worst is over.

The Ten of Swords at first glance appears to be an unpleasant card, but that is the nature of Tarot. Some cards are good and others bad and it would be dishonest to paint all cards as perfect. However, Tens represent the end of the element of any given suit, whether it is a good ending or bad. It is important to remember here that the keyword is "ending." Indeed, this card symbolizes that any unfortunate events are coming to an end and closure is in sight. Sadly, sometimes things do just go wrong and this may very well be the case. But do not lose hope because this card symbolizes the tail end of any disastrous series of events. This card also symbolizes any longed-for or long-awaited change. Moving on from this point could make you more positive and competent. Things can only get better.

- Sometimes it all goes wrong; it's over now, so time to move on.

Keywords (Reversed): Adaptation to environment, unconventional approaches, break hard habits

Ill Dignified or Reversed – Only an illusionary lifting of burdens or release from afflictions, as troubles may continue. Sometimes, depending on surrounding cards, death or fierce and extreme change. Only temporary good fortune.

The Ten of Swords reversed is not the most pleasant of cards to have in a spread. Whereas it's upright version is equally unpleasant, it does signify the nail in the coffin of any suffering. However, when it reverses, there may be the illusion that burdens are lifting, but the misery with this card just seems to drag on. Imagine when this card turns upside down. All ten swords fall down, but their blades point upwards seeking to impale anyone who stumbles onto them. If anyone should be unfortunate enough to fall onto the sharp blades, they won't just find themselves impaled, they will also slide painfully down them, thus prolonging the agony. The image is not a nice one, and sadly neither is this particular card whether it is upright or reversed. This present period may just be a difficult one for you; summon up all of your faith and courage and heave yourself off the figurative swords that are impaling you. Once you realize that any bad situations must eventually conclude, you will know that any mistakes along the way are not to be repeated. Hard habits are difficult to break but you need to do this in order to move onwards and upwards. Keep the faith.

- When at the bottom and feeling low, upwards is the only way to go.

Page Swords
The Princess of the Rushing Winds
The Lotus of the Palace of Air

NUMERICAL VALUE	7
ELEMENT	Air
ELEMENTAL NAME	Earth of Air
TETRAGRAMMATRON	Vau (Stabilization of Form)
HAIR COLOR	Light Brown
EYE COLOR	Blue
LIFE ASPECT	Intellectual Activity
ASTROLOGICAL ASSOCIATIONS	Gemini, Libra, Aquarius

Guideline Divinatory Meanings:

Keywords (Upright): Messages, information, endings, possibly journeys by plane

Upright – A good personal emissary, although sometimes a card associated with spying or surveying others from a detached viewpoint. A person of grace and dexterity, diplomatic and skilled in the ability to work out the true nature of things. A person who can negotiate expertly on behalf of his peers. Detachment is one of the true qualities of this figure.

The Page of Swords when read as a person in a spread is someone who would normally be less than 21 years of age and either male or female. This is someone who is quite skilful and knowledgeable, but also someone who should be careful not to become too complacent. If you are in the process of negotiating contracts or making business decisions, then the Page of Swords may present themselves as someone who can act as a person of insight to you in these areas. However, with this card in your spread, there is an indication that you need to be subtle in any approaches that you may decide to take. This card also symbolizes the receiving of highly anticipated news. If you are already in a relationship, then the Page of Swords suggests that simply dreaming about a situation rather than practical efforts may not necessarily be the way forward. The Page of Swords in your reading as a whole suggests that you should look out for news relating to any problems that you may have, as the answer is on its way.

- Hair light brown and eyes so blue, this person, is a friend to you.

Keywords (Reversed): Prying, duality, cunning, unforeseen events

Ill Dignified or Reversed – A two-faced, cunning and possibly vindictive person, with an inability to grasp the nettle. A seeker of hidden weaknesses in enemies, devious and given to snooping in other people's affairs. May be an indication of unforeseen events, health-related issues, or plans being overtaken by events.

The Page of Swords reversed is not such a nice character as when he is in his upright position. Instead of being the lovable, chatty fresh-faced teenager, this is someone who you really can't trust to keep a secret. Not only is he prone to letting the cat of out of the bag, he is also a bit of a nosey sort and given to prying. When he is around, beware of his/her false flattery, as it's quite possible that while professing adoration for you, he/she is in fact simply rooting out any of your hidden weaknesses. When this card turned upside down, he/she was badly scratched by his/her falling blade and this has left him/her rather sore. This card in its upright position can signify happy and welcome news. But the only

SWORDS

letters that this reversed Page will bring will be of the poison pen type. Don't expect anything cheery from him. Should you come across this card reversed in your spread, offer him a bandage for his wound but then send him packing swiftly on his way. This is not a nice character to have around. He/she is just the type to be really nice to your face but you wouldn't like what he/she says behind your back.

- Hair light brown and eyes so blue, this nosey soul, is spying on you.

Knight Swords

Lord of the Winds and the Breezes
King of the Spirits of Air

NUMERICAL VALUE	4
ELEMENT	Air
ELEMENTAL NAME	Fire of Air
TETRAGRAMMATRON	Vau (Stabilization of Form)
HAIR COLOR	Dark
EYE COLOR	Dark
LIFE ASPECT	Intellectual Activity
ASTROLOGICAL ASSOCIATIONS	Gemini, Libra, Aquarius

Guideline Divinatory Meanings:

Keywords (Upright): Travel, possibly by plane, decisive action, the archetypal warrior, defence, promotion

Upright – A clever, skilful and active person, courageous and strong, always at his best in a difficult situation. He may have a tendency to dominate, and depending upon surrounding cards, his movement may be either in or out of the querent's life for either better or worse. He is the Archetypal warrior.

The Knight of Swords is usually depicted by a Knight with his sword in a charging position, and this suggests that decisive action may be the best way forward. In terms of a person, this card indicates that someone is in or coming into your life who is most probably over 21 years of age. This is a person who gets easily bored and wants action. They may even have a tendency to take risks and can be very blasé about any danger. Indeed, they may appear to have no fear of the unknown. This person is also at their best in difficult situations, but you must be careful not to let this person take over. However, the Knight of Swords also represents direct action and making choices without a lot of time to think about all of the options. It may well be that you are about to be offered a chance at something by a quick-witted and impulsive person, but beware as this opportunity and the person offering it, may not stay focused in your direction.

- Eyes and hair so very dark; if you are the powder keg, he is the spark.

Keywords (Reversed): Disagreements, underhandedness

Ill Dignified or Reversed – Someone who is impetuous, sly, and deceitful, fierce in action with little staying power. A starter but not a finisher of things. Quarrels may be indicated, but this depends upon surrounding cards. Application of great force and energy becomes "simple-minded indulgence."

The Knight of Swords reversed is a card symbolic of someone who is impetuous, sly, and false hearted. Just like his metaphorical younger brother, the Page of Swords reversed, this Knight reversed is not only a hypocrite, he/she can be positively vindictive. When this card reverses upside down, his falling sword didn't just wound him, it chopped off his leg, leaving him very bitter indeed. He is very quick to react and to take action, but minus one leg, he just doesn't have a lot of staying power. In some instances, he can be portrayed as someone who may have learning difficulties, but in others he uses his keen knowledge negatively. He has quite a few negative traits and is someone who you probably could do without in your social circle. He is cunning and he can also symbolize underhanded dealings in your affairs. Watch out for anyone like this around you. Speaking wholly metaphorically, should this reversed card appear in your spread, don't offer this Knight a bandage, as you may have once offered the reversed Page of Swords. This time you should figuratively chop off his other leg to make sure he can't chase after you. Keep away from any characters who may be acting maliciously in your affairs and try not to start projects that you can't finish.

- Hair so dark, the same as eyes, steer clear this person, if you're wise.

Queen Swords
The Queen of the Thrones of Air

NUMERICAL VALUE	4
ELEMENT	Air
ELEMENTAL NAME	Water of Air
TETRAGRAMMATRON	Vau (Stabilization of Form)
HAIR COLOR	Light Brown
EYE COLOR	Gray
LIFE ASPECT	Intellectual Activity
ASTROLOGICAL ASSOCIATIONS	Gemini, Libra, Aquarius

Guideline Divinatory Meanings:

Keywords (Upright): Wisdom, attention to detail, balance

Upright – A complex, courageous, intelligent woman, who may well have suffered some deep sorrow or loss. She is concerned with attention to accuracy and detail and can skillfully balance opposing factions to meet her own needs. She has attained inner wisdom and a sense of truth. The card is one for women who have overcome adversity, especially at the hands of men, to obtain a state of grace. The ability of women.

The Queen of Swords is often represented by a Queen holding a sword in an upright position which indicates clarity of thought. This card represents a lady who has a deep understanding of things. She can "walk the walk" and "talk the talk" and is more than comfortable with her peers. She can talk knowledgeably with anyone, even the most intelligent among us. She is a sponge that soaks up information and can easily retell it in an easy-to-understand way. She would probably fare well in a consultancy role or maybe a teaching career. She has a keen eye for detail, can skillfully negotiate situations to her advantage, and has an inner wisdom, but she also stands out in the crowd. When the Queen of Swords appears in a spread, she can indicate a need to be steadfast in any approaches to situations. In order to ensure a clear perspective on things, think about your feelings and emotions and exactly what it is that you want. In terms of relationships, a person may be having problems committing themselves, as it is possible that what they have endured in the past may be holding them back in the present.

- Hair light brown and eyes of gray, this sharp-witted lady, won't stand in your way.

Keywords (Reversed): Transgression, intolerance, a card of misdeed

Ill Dignified or Reversed – Sorrow for the sake of sorrow. A card of wrongdoing as a reply to adverse circumstances. A deceitful, sly, intolerant, and narrow-minded woman, expert in the use of half truths and quiet slander. A formidable enemy due to her subtlety and sharp intellect.

The Queen of Swords reversed, just like her two metaphorical sons, the Page and Knight of Swords reversed, doesn't have a particularly nice personality, either. Words like *sly* and *vindictive* can apply to her in equal measure. She makes for a formidable opponent, particularly if she pops up in a business setting. This is a lady who has a sharp intellect, and because she knows the art of subtlety, it is not a good idea to cross swords with her. In the role of a mother-in-law, she would be represented as bossy, extremely domineering, and hypocritical. When this Queen of Swords reversed, her blade sliced into her skin leaving scars. These scars, although hidden, are deep, yet still surface through her misanthropic personality. When this card reversed shows up in a spread, the best course of action is to help her politely back onto her throne. This is a lady not to be tangled with. Trying to beat her is not an option, as she is a very malicious, driven, and a strong opponent. The best course of action here is to try not to ruffle her feathers; accept that in this argument it is probably better not to try to have the last word. Avoidance of conflict with this person is altogether better.

- Eyes of gray and hair light brown, this interfering tyrant, will get you down.

King Swords
The Prince of the Chariots of the Winds

NUMERICAL VALUE	4
ELEMENT	Air
ELEMENTAL NAME	Air of Air
TETRAGRAMMATRON	Vau (Stabilization of Form)
HAIR COLOR	Dark Brown
EYE COLOR	Dark
LIFE ASPECT	Intellectual Activity
ASTROLOGICAL ASSOCIATIONS	Gemini, Libra, Aquarius

Guideline Divinatory Meanings:

Keywords (Upright): Action, achievement, new projects, advice

Upright – This king is certainly a ruler. He is a law-maker, someone with a rational, alert, and inventive mind. An advocate of law and order and modernity to the expense of tradition. He has a tendency to be somewhat overcautious and leaves one project quickly to start on another. A man of independent judgement and an achiever in what he does.

The King of Swords, as a person, is someone who will take the high moral ground even at the expense of friends and family. This King is very different to the King of Cups who would put his family and friends above everything else; indeed, the King of Swords expects everyone to stick to his very strict standards. In terms of a career, this card symbolizes someone who is related to the following: law, consultancy, or even a judge, politician, soldier, doctor, or musician. This person has a very rational and logical mind and is an advocate of law and order. If this card is in your spread, then it is possible that you may receive some help and advice from someone in a high position or a position of power. It is also possible that as long as this advice is heeded, then it may bear fruit. In relationship terms, this card indicates a clarity of thought and purpose that in turn leads to a "meeting of minds." This is a positive card, and whereas the Queens in a spread may bring forth the ideas, the Kings help to make things real. They are the ones who break free from the constraints of the castle gates and forge ahead.

- Hair dark brown, eyes dark too, here's a man who's useful to you.
- This card is also known as "Dr. Death," the card of the Surgeon – the "Surgeon who wields his knife."

Keywords (Reversed): Meanness, scorn, undeserving aims, bad intentions

Ill Dignified or Reversed – The probability of great disruption and contempt for the weak. An abuse of power and authority. A calculating, obstinate man, capable of utmost malevolence to achieve his aims and desires.

The King of Swords reversed in the personality stakes can go one step further than his metaphorical wife, The Queen of Swords reversed, and her two sons reversed, the Knight and Page. As the degree of malice increases up the figurative bloodline, we end with The King of Swords reversed. In pursuit of knowledge and intellectual goals, this reversed King can sometimes be positively evil and sadistic. When he fell upside down on his sword, it caused a wound so deep that goodness flowed from it leaving an empty, embittered, and battle-hardened soul. When cunning fails him, he simply turns to brute force and he is given to bullying. He has an innate contempt for weakness and abuse of power is the norm for him. In battle on your side, he would make an excellent companion, but a ruthless and sadistic opponent on the other side. However, unlike his Queen reversed, confrontation, rather than appeasement, is a better way forward for you with such a character. As he is wounded when he falls upside down, use this opportunity to exploit his moment of weakness. In other words, don't run away from anyone acting with malice in your affairs; instead, pick your moment carefully and you are more likely to get a hearing.

- Eyes are dark and so is hair, a ruthless man, who is seldom fair.

Ace Coins
The Root of the Powers of Earth

NUMERICAL VALUE	5
SEASON	Winter
DIRECTION	North
ELEMENT	Earth
TETRAGRAMMATRON	Heh – Final (Completion of Energy into Form)
LIFE ASPECT	Money and Material
ASTROLOGICAL ASSOCIATIONS	Taurus, Capricorn, Virgo

Guideline Divinatory Meanings:

Keywords (Upright): Action, achievement, new projects, advice

Upright – Financial change for the better, material comfort, physical wellbeing, wealth, possessions, and an appreciation of the good things in life. The essence and luxury of the element of Earth.

The Ace of Coins is a very positive card to have in a spread. It indicates that all of the conditions are right to move ahead. The Ace of Coins has been likened to The Magician who presents his gifts to the fool to enable him to progress on his journey. Therefore, a helpful way to think of this card is that you may receive or already have all of the prerequisites to success. How you use this energy and great "vibe" is up to you, but this card indicates that everything is there to make things work well. Business is particularly well starred and personal relationships should do well and be harmonious. You may even find that you may come into contact with someone who leaves quite an impression on you. Material success and promotion are also associated with this card. Certainly with this card in your spread, you should have all of the elements of success around you, but you must manage everything well, as even positives have pitfalls as well as high points.

- Financial change all starts well; the till is full and the coffers swell.

Keywords (Reversed): Materialism, miserliness, avarice

Ill Dignified or Reversed – Greed, dependence upon physical pleasures for happiness, avarice, miserliness, and materialism. Lack of imagination and fear of death.

The Ace of Coins reversed is a stark contrast to its upright counterpart. If Aces are the spark of energy required to start something new, when this Ace falls to the floor, its coin becomes completely lost down a crack in the pavement. In other words, there may be a good venture to be started. However, if there is any doubt over the profitability of the venture, then it would be shelved before it was even given a chance to begin. When the Ace of Coins reversed shows up, money becomes the key. Everything begins to revolve around money and materialism; miserliness and avarice are all starred. This could be that you are feeling a little "tight" with your money at present or someone around you is. This card reversed also symbolizes disappointments regarding money. It suggests that if you were anticipating some extra cash coming your way, then there is a good chance that this won't materialize. With this card comes a warning not to get too absorbed in the pursuit of money beyond everything else. There is more to life than money and spiritual wellbeing is also important. When all you have in your life is purely of the material, the thought of death and losing all you have can become a frightening thought. Now may be a good time to broaden your spiritual awareness and don't end up like Scrooge. Don't go digging down the crack to find that lost coin. It may serve better to leave it there for someone less fortunate than you to find.

- If you find yourself being greedy, now's the time to think of the needy.

II Coins
The Lord of Harmonious Change

NUMERICAL VALUE	2
ELEMENT	Earth
TETRAGRAMMATRON	Heh – Final (Completion of Energy into Form)
LIFE ASPECT	Money and Material
ASTROLOGICAL ASSOCIATIONS	Taurus, Capricorn, Virgo

Guideline Divinatory Meanings:

Keywords (Upright): Decisions, choices, changes

Upright – Vast change and fluctuations. A need to balance many skills when planning ahead. A warning against purchasing items on credit. The card indicates: imminent changes and movement, such as news, journeys, communications, money, and material preoccupations. All change must be skillfully navigated with knowledgeable manipulation of life's rules, in order to attain continued success. There needs to be careful handling of established business.

The Two of Coins is a positive card and suggests that your circumstances, particularly financial circumstances, are likely to change, hopefully for the better. This is a card all about juggling and then getting the balance right in your life. You may find that with this card in your spread, there are a lot of changes on the horizon, as it is associated with changes and movement, such as news, journeys, communications, money, and material preoccupations. You may find that you are juggling a number of these "balls" at once, but at some point, you will need to make choices that will lead to the balance and harmony you require. Everyone knows what happens when they have too many balls in the air at once. There may be decisions to be made regarding two alternatives, monetary decisions, or even job opportunities. Be prepared to take advantage of any opportunities that may present themselves to you. In terms of relationships, then again, as this is a card of decisions, then you may be faced with choices to make regarding the next stage of a relationship. This may or may not involve spending some cash.

- Now might be the time to juggle, in order to avoid a financial struggle.

Keywords (Reversed): Over-indulgence, physical pleasures, any warnings should be heeded

Ill Dignified or Reversed – Fecklessness, reckless elation, and discounting warnings of impending trouble. Debt. May also indicate over-indulgence in physical pleasures or drunkenness. Inability to complete a project.

The Two of Coins reversed is about a loss of focus. The Two of Coins upright is a card of juggling things to keep the balance right. You have two figurative coins in the air and you are juggling to keep them there. However, when this card reverses, even a momentary lapse of concentration can lead to the two coins falling to the floor and rolling away. This card offers a warning against taking on too much debt and general over-indulgence. Taking your eye off the ball will lead to those figurative coins falling away, so you need to keep focused if you want to bring any projects to a successful conclusion. Don't let a cold attitude hamper any relationships. To succeed here you need to re-focus, get your eye back on the ball, find the lost coins and start to juggle them again.

- Keep your eye on the ball, or risk a bank balance fall.

III Coins
The Lord of Material Works

NUMERICAL VALUE	3
ELEMENT	Earth
TETRAGRAMMATRON	Heh – Final (Completion of Energy into Form)
LIFE ASPECT	Money and Material
ASTROLOGICAL ASSOCIATIONS	Taurus, Capricorn, Virgo

Guideline Divinatory Meanings:

Keywords (Upright): Expansion, development, success

Upright – Success gained through hard work and effort. A gain in commerce and an increase in material things. This is the card of the businessman, craftsman, and merchant. Skilful work is both awarded and appreciated. A good time to start a project, with an indication of help in business.

The Three of Coins is a card of growth and development. This is a card of the tradesman, craftsman, and business person. It is symbolic of hard work that is finally beginning to pay off. It suggests that any planning is starting to bear fruit and ideas are coming to fruition. As long as all of the right decisions have been made and all of the correct plans put in place, now may be a good time to start a new project, as business can be well starred with this card. This card is also indicative of recognition for hard work and you may find that all your previous efforts will finally be rewarded with the recognition that they deserve. With regards to health, this card can be indicative of positive results as a result of any new exercise regimes or therapy. In terms of relationships, the card signifies that you may want to make the effort to build and/or maintain a relationship. Or it could be that someone wants to do that within your relationship. Either way, this is generally a positive card to have in your spread, particularly if you have been working hard lately.

- Now's the time for a period of growth, an increase in wealth, or maybe both.

Keywords (Reversed): Missed opportunities, unrewarding effort, unrewarding work

Ill Dignified or Reversed – Miserliness, missed opportunities through fear of loss, inability to benefit from the advice of others as a result of obstinacy, conceit or prejudice. Effort that yields disappointing results.

The Three of Coins reversed deals with hard work that proves to be unrewarding. It is also a card of a sloppy apprentice or sloppy workmanship. When this card reverses and the coins fall to the floor, they don't bounce as might be expected; instead, they smash into tiny pieces, showing how badly made they were in the first place. When this card reversed appears in a spread, it may be a good time to examine whether or not projects are progressing as they should. If all of your efforts are being ploughed into, something that you feel is not very fruitful, then maybe it is time to listen to advice and quit while you are ahead. Try not to ignore any helpful advice and guard against preconceived ideas and prejudices.

- When hard work shows a loss instead, it's time to quit while you're ahead.

IV Coins
The Lord of Earthly Power

NUMERICAL VALUE	4
ELEMENT	Earth
TETRAGRAMMATRON	Heh – Final (Completion of Energy into Form)
LIFE ASPECT	Money and Material
ASTROLOGICAL ASSOCIATIONS	Taurus, Capricorn, Virgo

Guideline Divinatory Meanings:

Keywords (Upright): Financial security, consolidation, solid foundations

Upright – Financial and material security. An increase in power and authority in business, through influence and wealth. Business and monetary obstacles will be overcome. Promotion. Force is not needed to achieve law and order; it can be done through negotiation.

The Four of Coins is symbolic of financial and material security and being in a comfortable position where you can easily live within your means. However, this card also indicates that there may be a tendency towards materialism and possibly even a touch of miserliness creeping into your situation. This card suggests that now you have saved up or reached a comfortable financial position, you want to hang onto it at all costs. When this card appears it also suggests that you may possibly be in a position of status, health, wealth, and material comfort and you really do want to hang onto all of this. However, sometimes clinging onto something so hard can bring its own set of problems. Perhaps now is the time to look to the really important things in life, such as family and friends and share the good luck with everyone. There is a warning to try to guard against selfish behavior, and if you are in a relationship, try not to let materialism overthrow more emotional values. In terms of relationships, generally this card warns that selfishness and materialism on either side of the partnership could prove problematic. In order for the relationship to develop, the people involved must remain open to changes and new ideas. Sharing and caring are probably the best watch words here.

- Financial security feels just right, keep it close, and hold it tight.
- The "Miser" card.

Keywords (Reversed): Bureaucracy, lack of ability to delegate, greediness

Ill Dignified or Reversed – Lack of an ability to delegate work, bureaucracy that destroys individual initiative. Greed. A fear of losing that which is familiar and established, which in turn makes for opposition to change.

The Four of Coins reversed can represent two extremes. When this card reverses, there is an option to hang onto the four coins so that they aren't lost as they tumble; or conversely the other option is to throw away those coins and save yourself as you fall. But either way, neither option is an ideal solution. When this card shows up, there is a warning to guard against worrying too much about losing all that you have achieved. Sometimes, change is good as well, and a fear of losing the well established should not become a barrier to trying something new. Where work-related matters are concerned, try not to fear the delegation of work. Just because you need to delegate does not automatically mean that you will lose all you have worked for to date. At the other extreme, this card can warn against throwing away what you have worked for. In this instance, the guidance is not to be too profligate, too lax with money, and to beware of taking on too much debt. The best way forward with the Four of Coins reversed is to strike a balance in your affairs. When the four coins begin to fall as they reverse, it may be better to hang on to a couple, but let the others go, so you can also break your fall. This is a more balanced approach, rather than clinging onto everything for dear life and ruining your health in the process.

- When you're acting like a miser, be more generous, that's much wiser.

V Coins
The Lord of Material Trouble

NUMERICAL VALUE	5
ELEMENT	Earth
TETRAGRAMMATRON	Heh – Final (Completion of Energy into Form)
LIFE ASPECT	Money and Material
ASTROLOGICAL ASSOCIATIONS	Taurus, Capricorn, Virgo

Guideline Divinatory Meanings:

Keywords (Upright): Profligacy, money issues, change, a need for wise spending

Upright – Redundancy, loss of financial stability, material worries, lack of wealth. A warning of money troubles lying ahead; however, there is a suggestion that restriction in certain areas may open doors in others. Avenues yet to be explored, a message of not being too despondent.

The Five of Coins is not a great card to have in your spread with regards to money. It warns that there may be material and financial worries on the horizon. This card can also signify a low point and in many respects it is a lonely card of change that financially speaking may not always be positive. However, the best way to tackle this card is to recognize that although it is a sad and lonely card, you are not really alone and in your life you have much to be happy about. Indeed, although there is no denying that this card symbolizes issues relating to the material and financial aspects of your life, this is no great loss. The reason for this is that you still have the spiritual side to your life; and although now may be a low point, things from here can only get better financially, because where there is life, there is always hope. It is important with this card in your spread not to miss out on any opportunities for advancement. If you already have a job, it can indicate that you are finding your work a little boring and uninteresting at the moment. In terms of a relationship, there is some indication of possible separation from a partner and this may be linked to money problems. What must be taken from this card is that it is symbolic of a low point and you must realize that this could be your low point from where things can and only will get better.

- Financially now, it's not great; it will improve, but you'll have to wait.

Keywords (Reversed): Careful financial planning, monetary issues, overindulgence

Ill Dignified or Reversed – Long-term job seeking. Lack of success. Sometimes poverty and destitution. Adversity that may be overcome were it not for a lack of imagination or the ability to be less obstinate.

The Five of Coins reversed is a card that warns that, when in a hole, stop digging. In its upright position, this card is not the greatest card to have when relating to money. Indeed when this card reverses, all of the coins drop to the floor and roll quickly away. There is no money left. When there is no money at all left, then it is not wise to continue spending, because spending money that you don't have is always eventually a recipe for disaster. This card warns that prudence is the watch word here. Careful financial planning is required if complete monetary meltdown is to be avoided. The key with this card is to ensure that you plan out all of your finances carefully. Instead of waiting until this card reverses, makes sure that you have a safety net in place beforehand. In that way, you can ensure that you can catch those falling coins before they all roll away from you. In other words, always plan to have a monetary reserve and never spend what you don't have.

- When the wolf is at the door, sort your finances, or he'll want more.

VI Coins
The Lord of Material Success

NUMERICAL VALUE	6
ELEMENT	Earth
TETRAGRAMMATRON	Heh – Final (Completion of Energy into Form)
LIFE ASPECT	Money and Material
ASTROLOGICAL ASSOCIATIONS	Taurus, Capricorn, Virgo

Guideline Divinatory Meanings:

Keywords (Upright): Social occasions, friendly criticism, original ideas, creative partnerships

Upright – Solvency in material affairs, clearance of debts, and use of good fortune to the benefit of others. Repayment of favors. Charity, patronage, sympathy, and a kind heart.

The Six of Coins is a card all about the restoration of balance and harmony through charity and the giving and receiving of material and financial gifts. This card symbolizes wealth in one corner that is put into or made available to the hands of the deserving and needy. A good analogy for this card is when someone who has too much money for tax purposes goes on to give that money to charity. In doing so, balance is restored and two problems are solved at once through the act of giving, serving a mutual purpose. In terms of this card in your spread, it can indicate a time when you will reap the rewards of any hard efforts you may make. Business projects are well starred. Indeed, this card suggests the sowing of some nice seeds and being generous and kind, which in turn through the laws of Karma, will make sure that you reap nice rewards.

- When you choose to be kind, all manner of happiness you will give and find.
- The "Generosity" card.

Keywords (Reversed): Financial issues, suppression

Ill Dignified or Reversed – Reckless and careless behavior with money. Loss of money through carelessness, deceit or theft. Extravagance.

The Six of Coins reversed serves as a warning to be very careful with money right now, because currently you may not feel like you have much of it. In its upright position, it is all about balance and harmony gained through charity and the sharing of material and financial gifts with the needy and deserving. When this card reverses, however, it is very similar to the Five of Coins reversing, in that all of the coins roll away and disappear. Sadly though, this time, a couple of thieves grab these coins, ensuring that there's no way of you getting them back. Even if you are feeling generous at present, you are unable to give out any cash because you simply don't have it. You may have lost it through reckless or careless behavior, but then again maybe it was stolen from you or possibly you were conned out of it. The upright version of this card also hints that there may be someone waiting in the wings to make a kindly financial gesture. However, this is not so with the Six of Coins reversed; no one is going to be charitable or give you a free lunch. Therefore, when this card reversed shows up in a spread, keep your hand firmly on your wallet, not only to stop yourself from spending, but also to stop any unwelcome light fingers dipping in there. When this card falls upside down, grab those coins before they have chance to roll away.

- Now's the time to hang onto your lot, it isn't much, but it's all you've got.

VII Coins
The Lord of Success Unfulfilled

NUMERICAL VALUE	7
ELEMENT	Earth
TETRAGRAMMATRON	Heh – Final (Completion of Energy into Form)
LIFE ASPECT	Money and Material
ASTROLOGICAL ASSOCIATIONS	Taurus, Capricorn, Virgo

Guideline Divinatory Meanings:

Keywords (Upright): Never surrender, beware complacency, intellectual victory, news

Upright – Promising projects that fail. A warning not to rest upon one's laurels, as success is only attainable through continued hard work. Material success may be possible, but the nettle must be grasped. Previous past effort wasted through inertia in the present. Reaping no reward from charitable work.

The Seven of Coins is all about taking back control of a situation and using your skill and judgment to put the balance back into your life. You may be feeling that some things are out of your control at the moment, but the best thing to do here is to be patient and wait for things to develop. There is a warning that comes with this card which suggests that if promising projects are not to fail, then you must not be complacent about success and rest on your laurels. Only continued hard work will ensure a positive outcome. This card has been likened to someone who put in the groundwork, tucked away their savings, and now needs to sit back and wait for interest rates to go up. What has been achieved has been achieved and now it is out of your hands; just like you have no control over interest rates, you must sit back and be patient and wait for a favorable outcome. Now is the time to plan carefully for your future; for example, you may like to do a further course of study, take a holiday or maybe even change direction at work. The Seven of Coins is all about a steady journey towards your goals. This card also indicates that you may receive some help or encouraging news. As long as you have put in all of the necessary groundwork, then there should also be steady progress regarding financial affairs and maybe even a favor returned.

- Now is the time to be patient and wait; things go well, it's your fate.
- The "Waiting" card.

Keywords (Reversed): Gambling, risky businesses, money issues

Ill Dignified or Reversed – Self inflicted money worries. Possibly insolvency, gambling and promising circumstances that end in failure. Financial insecurity.

The Seven of Coins reversed is a card of impatience, if its upright card is the "Waiting" card, then this card is where "only fools rush in." It is about trying to "make a fast buck." Whether this is by risk taking or gambling or playing the stock market, none of these actions are advised right now. When the Seven of Coins reverse, they fall in a heap on the roulette table, ready to be placed as a bet. This is risky. If the numbers don't come up, then you will be left with some self-induced money worries. When this card reversed shows up in a spread, then the advice is to snatch up those figurative coins from the roulette table and plan more carefully how you can make the money work for you. It may be a case of investing in a bank account. This may not be the fastest way to earn some extra cash, but it is a lot safer than indulging in more risky ventures. Patience and self discipline are the ways to tackle this card when it appears.

- Patience and waiting take their toll; better this way, than a dice's roll.

VIII Coins
The Lord of Prudence

NUMERICAL VALUE	8
ELEMENT	Earth
TETRAGRAMMATRON	Heh – Final (Completion of Energy into Form)
LIFE ASPECT	Money and Material
ASTROLOGICAL ASSOCIATIONS	Taurus, Capricorn, Virgo

Guideline Divinatory Meanings:

Keywords (Upright): Perseverance, empowerment, talent, continued effort

Upright – The use of one's skills and personal interests to rewarding and profitable ends. Reaping the fruits of one's labour, a small increase in money. An advantageous card for any talented or enthusiastic individuals. To enjoy lasting success efforts should be continuous and not halted prematurely. Thriftiness.

The Eight of Coins is sometimes referred to as the card of the apprentice, as it is a card about starting over or beginning to learn about something new. This card is symbolic of finding one's feet in a situation and starting at the bottom and working one's way up. Just as an apprentice might begin by sweeping the floors, there is always the possibility of bettering yourself even though the current situation may be frustrating and you may find that you have made mistakes. The idea here with this card in your spread, suggests that you are building foundations for success in the future. Indeed, with continual hard work and keeping up your motivation, your efforts should pay off. This card also symbolizes possibilities regarding new skills and maybe even new job opportunities. You might even be considering some kind of course that may broaden your career opportunities. Even if you have been thrown in at the deep end, learn all that you can and keep on swimming as your desired destination is within your reach.

- Learning or starting something new, make your talents, work for you.
- The "Apprentice" card.

Keywords (Reversed): Financial legalities, perseverance, energies misused

Ill Dignified or Reversed – Inappropriate use of energy and skills for unsuitable ends. Underhanded dealings in business affairs. Short-term gain at the expense of long-term profit.

The Eight of Coins reversed suggests that hard work, effort, and patience are the only way to win out in a situation. The Eight of Coins in the upright position is sometimes referred to as the apprentice card and it is about starting at the bottom and working your way up. However, there is no new beginning with this card; this is not a card of an enthusiastic apprentice starting out on his/her chosen career. The Eight of Coins reversed is more suited to someone who has been in a business for a while and maybe wants a change or a quick fix to this problem. When this card reverses, the eight coins don't immediately drop. Instead, they cling desperately to the wall. Rather than wait until all of the coins eventually fall into your lap (the ultimate prize), you dash away with the first one that comes loose. In other words, you grab at short-term gain at the expense of longer-term profit. This card reversed tells that there is no quick-and-easy route to riches and any dishonest business dealings should be avoided at all costs. There is also an indication with this card that you may be feeling a little bored with your job. Therefore, when this reversed card shows up, the best course of action is to "get stuck in," pick up a figurative hammer, and knock the rest of the coins to the floor. In other words, the only way to win with this card is to accept that you need to plan your future carefully and know that it will take time and perseverance to succeed.

- Slow and steady wins the race; this is a truth, you have to face.

Hidden Meaning: The Eight of Coins together with the Five of Cups may signify upset with a dark haired person.

IX Coins
The Lord of Material Gain

NUMERICAL VALUE	9
ELEMENT	Earth
TETRAGRAMMATRON	Heh – Final (Completion of Energy into Form)
LIFE ASPECT	Money and Material
ASTROLOGICAL ASSOCIATIONS	Taurus, Capricorn, Virgo

Guideline Divinatory Meanings:

Keywords (Upright): Sudden monetary gains, reassessment, unexpected gifts

Upright – The enjoyment of hard-earned success. Financial gains made from unexpected sources, such as: monetary gifts, winnings, inheritances, and settlements. Unearned income, possibly from a divorce settlement. Popularity, common sense, and order arising out of chaos.

The Nine of Coins is a good card to have in your spread from a monetary point of view, as it suggests a nice little windfall or payment that has come from a "nice little earner" or bonus for work well done. This card indicates some monetary gain usually from an unexpected source. If the windfall does come to pass, then this card is symbolic of being able to afford what you heart desires and what typically may have been out of your reach. It is a card of luxury and having some of life's little treats; for example, some time away in a luxury hotel or simply going to a spa. Whatever it is you want, should you manage to obtain it, then this card suggests that it will make you happy. Any business decisions that may have arisen out of business negotiations should prove positive and successful. Any success achieved should make you feel content. Certainly having the means to experience a little bit of what you fancy will do you no harm.

- Wealth and fortune has been found, happiness and mirth is all around.
- The "Rich Bitch" card.

Keywords (Reversed): Uncertainty, bills, questionable means, and actions

Ill Dignified or Reversed – Affluence obtained via dubious practices. Theft, swindling, and pilfering. Corruption and success earned from the backs and misfortunes of others. This card also warns that present calm and stability will not be sustained.

The Nine of Coins reversed suggests that financially all in the garden may not be rosy. The Nine of Coins upright is a good card to have in a spread and tells of "nice little earners" or windfalls. However, reverse this card and the opposite may be true. This could be a time of unexpected bills, and at its worst, complete financial instability from a once-firm monetary base. When this card turns upside down, the once-ordered coins fall into disarray on the floor. Where stability stood, chaos now reigns. Regardless of your current financial situation, and even if material security is compromised, there is a warning against wealth obtained by questionable means. Dubious practices lead to financial ruin. When this card reversed appears, it is a time to expect the unexpected regarding bills and finances. Going back to the figurative coins lying in disarray on the floor, stack them neatly in the corner (order from chaos). Pile them high and make sure you save them up for that rainy day.

- When the cupboard seems all bare, sometimes life, just doesn't feel fair.

X Coins
The Lord of Wealth

NUMERICAL VALUE	10
ELEMENT	Earth
TETRAGRAMMATRON	Heh – Final (Completion of Energy into Form)
LIFE ASPECT	Money and Material
ASTROLOGICAL ASSOCIATIONS	Taurus, Capricorn, Virgo

Guideline Divinatory Meanings:

Keywords (Upright): Financial security, completion, some travel, gain

Upright – Emotional and financial stability. Family fortunes, inheritance, and prosperity that has been built up and handed down over the generations. The formation of family tradition. This card may indicate good fortune regarding a dowry.

The Ten of Coins, as is common with the Ten of any suit, represents the final element of that suit for good or for bad. In this case the Ten of Coins symbolizes the height of wealth and prosperity. This could take a variety of forms; for example, your mortgage may now be complete and the family home paid for, or you may be in for a lottery win, or trust fund that matures. Either way, this card symbolizes wealth, security, and contentment with emphasis on material success. However, in terms of a project, this card can indicate that projects could successfully complete and there may even be some opportunity for promotion or advancement at work. In terms of relationships, there may even be a relationship linked to work. Congenial family relations are starred and you could find yourself in a favorable position to help out any less fortunate family members. From a financial point of view, certainly this is a positive card to have in your spread as it is symbolic of wealth, gain, riches, material, and financial security within a family environment.

- Once the seeds have all been grown, wealth and happiness enter your home.

Keywords (Reversed): Family disagreements about money, negative effects of wealth

Ill Dignified or Reversed – The negative effects of vast wealth and the restrictive effects of long tradition. Family arguments about money, or the breaking up of an estate after a death. This card may also indicate burglary.

The Ten of Coins reversed is often symbolic of family disputes that are most likely linked to money. Imagine all ten coins falling to the floor and a big family scramble to pick them up. Instead of fairly sharing out the fallen coins, some relatives walk away with more than others, and ultimately, this unfair situation causes tensions to arise. This card is strongly linked to inheritance and family tradition. There are a few possibilities with this card. At best, it is about disputes over money and the sharing out of money among family. At worst, this card can signify that money that was expected from a will or dowry, may not only fail to materialize, but a pile of debts could be left to settle as well. This card reversed is also concerned with the negative effects of wealth. It warns against the squandering of an inheritance or the gambling away of it. When this card reversed appears, you may find that you are feeling trapped by any long-family traditions; this is not the best time for family harmony generally. When some of those figurative relatives get away with more coins than others, call them back into the room and negotiate a better deal for everyone. In other words, family in-fighting is not the way forward here; it is important that everyone gets their equal share.

- Money matters cause a row, the time for fighting is not now.

Page Coins

The Princess of the Echoing Hills
The Rose of the Palace of Earth

NUMERICAL VALUE	7
ELEMENT	Earth
ELEMENTAL NAME	Earth of Earth
TETRAGRAMMATRON	Heh – Final (Completion of Energy into Form)
HAIR COLOR	Rich Brown
EYE COLOR	Dark
LIFE ASPECT	Money and Material
ASTROLOGICAL ASSOCIATIONS	Taurus, Capricorn, Virgo

Guideline Divinatory Meanings:

Keywords (Upright): Study, advancement, learning, luck, messages about money

Upright – A meticulous, hardworking man, proud of his responsibilities. He is essentially honorable, a good administrator, but may sometimes be a little too diligent and overzealous in his duties.

The Page of Coins as with all of the court cards can represent a person. Usually, Pages are symbolic of younger people and that is the best way to think of them. As a personality, the Page of Coins is very hands on; in terms of children, they are the sort to get covered in dirt or start making mud pies. However, they are very focused on their goals and know how to work hard and save up in order to achieve their aims. But on the whole, they are kind hearted and generous and a lively personality to have around you. Of course, as well as representing a person, the Page of Coins also symbolizes messages about money and good fortune and a good unexpected improvement in health and wellbeing. This card may also represent research and study and any progress you may make could be achieved through learning. Good exam results are sometimes symbolized by this card.

- Hair rich brown and eyes so dark, this person is, a real bright spark.

Keywords (Reversed): Lack of humor, feelings of self importance, love of power

Ill Dignified or Reversed – A person with no sense of humor and full of his own importance. A person who enjoys the power he wields over those below him. Depending upon the surrounding cards, there may be some unwelcome news concerning monetary matters.

The Page of Coins reversed symbolizes someone who is given to being petty. They pick away and criticize tiny details without seeing the bigger picture. It is also a card of someone who enjoys wielding a certain amount of power over those below him. Unlike his upright self, he is somewhat unfocussed and lazy when it comes to getting anything done. When this card falls upside down, The Page of Coins falls to the floor and so does his coin. Unfortunately, he simply can't be bothered to pick it up off the floor and continues on his way, wandering off minus his coin or money, if you like. Therefore, when this card reversed shows up in your spread, it is unlikely that he will be bringing a gift of money or news of monetary gain. He is more likely to be bringing a demand for money, a bill, or a tax demand. The Page of Coins left his cash on the floor when he fell, so he had to borrow some along the way. For this reason, there is a warning to plan for any unwelcome news concerning money. In this scenario, you will be the one picking up the tab, or figuratively speaking, the coin that the Page left on the floor.

- Eyes so dark and hair rich brown, the news he brings may get you down.

Knight Coins

The Lord of the Wild and Fertile Land
The King of the Spirits of Earth

NUMERICAL VALUE	4
ELEMENT	Earth
ELEMENTAL NAME	Fire of Earth
TETRAGRAMMATRON	Heh – Final (Completion of Energy into Form)
HAIR COLOR	Dark Brown
EYE COLOR	Dark
LIFE ASPECT	Money and Material
ASTROLOGICAL ASSOCIATIONS	Taurus, Capricorn, Virgo

Guideline Divinatory Meanings:

Keywords (Upright): Travel on foot, a good provider, patience, hard work, thoughts about increasing wealth

Upright – An impassive, indifferent, and stoical person, who does not always appreciate the feelings of others. A very traditional person who is clever in monetary affairs, patient, and hardworking.

The Knight of Coins often represents someone who is hardworking and aims to achieve the best things in life. Although he may be aged anywhere from 21 to around 30 years of age, he may be somewhat emotionally immature. However, he knows exactly what he wants from life and is prepared to plan and work hard to get it. He is a character who likes his own space and hates it to be invaded. He may have any number of projects on the go at once, but all with a clear aim in mind. As well as the possibility that someone of this nature is going to cross your path, the Knight of Coins also symbolizes some form of travel, most probably on foot, and this could also include hiking, walking, and cycling. This card also represents a good provider. This may well be a time that you are feeling innovative, but with the Knight of Coins in your spread, he also ensures that you keep a logical perspective as well.

- Hair dark brown and dark eyes too, this hardworking Knight, will travel with you.

Keywords (Reversed): Financial inertia, a greedy person, monetary maneuverings

Ill Dignified or Reversed – A greedy and grasping person, sometimes self satisfied and smug. Depending upon the surrounding cards, may indicate that finances have reached a break-even point or even a standstill.

The Knight of Coins reversed is symbolic of someone who is out for himself or herself regarding money. They do not take kindly to the financial successes of others, as it can leave them quite jealous. When this Knight reverses, his horse falls and squashes his coin, so that it's not as shiny or straight as those of his friends. This causes him to be envious. The Page of Coins reversed is also the type of person to seem as if they are working really hard, but actually they are simply coasting. They are the type to pocket any change, look for a fast buck and they seldom leave tips. This is not the nicest person to have around when dealing with financial matters. When this card appears reversed, the best course of action is to straighten his coin and re-assure him that his money is just as good as everyone else's. In its upright position this card also represents some form of travel, most probably on foot. When this card is around make sure the Band-Aids are handy and plan your route well. A person like The Knight of Coins on a journey would be enough to put a damper on any day out.

- Hair dark brown and dark eyes, too, this young Knight, may be jealous of you.

Queen Coins
The Queen of the Thrones of Earth

NUMERICAL VALUE	4
ELEMENT	Earth
ELEMENTAL NAME	Water of Earth
TETRAGRAMMATRON	Heh – Final (Completion of Energy into Form)
HAIR COLOR	Dark
EYE COLOR	Dark
LIFE ASPECT	Money and Material
ASTROLOGICAL ASSOCIATIONS	Taurus, Capricorn, Virgo

Guideline Divinatory Meanings:

Keywords (Upright): Financial Security, making a business work, a woman of Libra temperament

Upright – A capable and practical businesswoman, who enjoys her material comforts. She has a responsible attitude to her wealth and uses it to advance the fortunes of those in her inner circle. She is neither particularly bright nor insightful, but has depth of feeling with an appreciation of life's pleasures.

The Queen of Coins, as with the other Queens in a deck, tends to be a card that helps to make things real. If you imagine that the Pages allow the seeds to be sown and the Knights spread the ideas, then the Queens help to, metaphorically speaking, bring forth that life. Indeed, the Queen of Coins is no exception, as she represents a very competent business woman who cares passionately about her family and friends and she will do all she can to further their careers or assist them generally. With this card in your spread, you may find that you come across a caring, sensitive person who is able and willing to give some sound business advice. As the Queen of Coins is also symbolic of status and financial security, it is possible that such a person may offer you assistance. If you are thinking about a new diet or exercise plan, then this is well starred. General success may well be achievable through the careful and practical implementation of your ideas.

- Hair so dark, and eyes, too, this caring woman, is an asset to you.

Keywords (Reversed): Sycophants, fear of criticism, suspicions, narrow-mindedness

Ill Dignified or Reversed – A person who enjoys the company of sycophants to shield her from criticism and uses her wealth to do this. She is unable to see beyond material possessions or rise above them. She can be highly changeable with a suspicious and narrow-minded outlook towards things that are either new or that she misunderstands. Fortune used for displays of grandeur and opulence.

The Queen of Coins is someone who has a love of material possessions. If she is not being particularly miserly, then she will be a complete spendthrift. When The Queen of Coins falls upside down, her throne and her coin become damaged in the fall. However, for this Queen reversed, repairs are not good enough. Instead, she goes out and spends copious amounts of money on replacing them. "If it isn't broke, then just buy a new one," is her motto. Her social circle is filled with sycophants and "yes men" who are awed by her material possessions. Deep and meaningful relationships are not her strong point as she hates any criticism. She also has very exacting standards and if she is capable of doing something then she looks unfavorably on anyone else who maybe can't. Therefore, this is someone who would make a demanding boss. In many respects, this Queen reversed is one who hides behind her wealth. She really struggles to see beyond the material side of life. Materialism, conflict, and insecurity are words that fit very well with this card. When you see her on the floor with her damaged throne and coin, take the time to explain, that actually, if it's broke, then fix it.

- Hair so dark and eyes, too, she hates secondhand, and only buys new.

King Coins
Prince of the Chariot of Earth

NUMERICAL VALUE	4
ELEMENT	Earth
ELEMENTAL NAME	Air of Earth
TETRAGRAMMATRON	Heh – Final (Completion of Energy into Form)
HAIR COLOR	Dark
EYE COLOR	Dark
LIFE ASPECT	Money and Material
ASTROLOGICAL ASSOCIATIONS	Taurus, Capricorn, Virgo

Guideline Divinatory Meanings:

Keywords (Upright): Planning, advice, counsel, promising ventures

Upright – A loyal and dependable leader who is neither particularly intelligent or imaginative. He is trustworthy, patient, cautious, and uses his inborn wisdom to increase his wealth. He is slow to lose his temper, but once angered, he stands rigid against his enemies.

The King of Coins is a loyal and dependable leader and someone who has worked hard all of his life to achieve his aims. He is slow to ask for favors, but will often offer them. Generally, he does not like to be indebted to anyone and is a particularly proud person. This respected man is likely to be a civil servant, draftsman, engineer, supervisor, farmer, or, surprisingly, even a performer. With this card in your spread, you may find yourself planning for a new business venture, or thinking about new and different ways of making money or designing something, you may even have thoughts about building a new house and home. Either way, this card symbolizes the achievement of goals through careful, practical planning, and effort. In terms of a relationship, this card indicates one which has all of the required material comforts where the partner associates contentment with material well-being. Watch out for someone who can give you financial/business advice and assistance, because this card in your spread suggests that they could be really helpful to you.

- Hair so dark and eyes, too, a loyal and dependable leader, who respects you.

Keywords (Reversed): Beauty blindness, dislike of change, a mercenary attitude

Ill Dignified or Reversed – A person who is easily bought, dull, very materialistic, and mercenary. He is blind to beauty and hates change as he finds it hard to adapt. He treads a well-worn path, even if it leads nowhere.

The King of Coins reversed is very similar in character to his Queen, i.e., The Queen of Coins reversed. He is overly preoccupied with money, and like his son, the Page of Coins reversed, he can become quite jealous if he sees that others have more than him. However, this card goes one further because he is also easily bought by money. He is insensitive and shallow, and in many respects, quite stupid. He treads a well-worn path and even if he is on a road to nowhere, he just blindly keeps on going. Whereas this card in his upright position is someone who can offer financial/business advice and assistance, this person in the reversed position is more likely to oppose you regarding any financial or work-related issues. When The King of Coins turned upside down, just like his Queen upside down, both his throne and coin were damaged, too. However, unlike the Queen reversed, his motto is, "Well if it ain't broke – don't fix it!" A *dodgy* throne and coin won't bother him as long as it doesn't involve spending money. When this card reversed shows up, then let The King know that just because it 'ain't' broke, it still might need to be fixed.

- Hair so dark and eyes, too, this mercenary man, will oppose you.

Additional Notes

There are Key themes that apply to the Minor Arcana cards and these are as follows:

KEY THEMES

CARD	THEME
Aces of any suit	New beginnings
Twos of any suit	Balance and choice
Threes of any suit	Growth and expansion of choices made
Fours of any suit	Stability
Fives of any suit	Tricky Karmic change
Sixes of any suit	Harmony and balance
Sevens of any suit	Wisdom and learning
Eights of any suit	Personal power (new faces, new places)
Nine of any suit	Reassessment, wishes, good luck and fate
Tens of any suit	Completion

IN A SPREAD:

Aces 4 Aces indicate power 3 Aces indicate wealth 2 Aces indicate moves	**Eights** 4 Eights indicate news 3 Eights indicate travel
Twos 4 Twos indicate conventions 3 Twos indicate reviews	**Nines** 4 Nines indicate responsibility 3 Nines indicate communication
Threes 4 Threes indicate tenacity and resoluteness 3 Threes indicate deception	**Tens** 4 Tens indicate worry 3 Tens indicate commerce
Fours 4 Fours indicate relaxation 3 Fours indicate enterprise	**Pages** 4 Pages indicate education 3 Pages indicate children 2 Pages indicate fun
Fives 4 Fives indicate arguments 3 Fives indicate peace	**Knights** 4 Knights indicate military 3 Knights indicate people 2 Knights indicate old friends
Sixes 4 Sixes indicate calm 3 Sixes indicate achievement	**Queens** 4 Queens indicate government 3 Queens indicate females and friends 2 Queens indicate defamation
Sevens 4 Sevens indicate disappointment 3 Sevens indicate contracts	**Kings** 4 Kings indicate world affairs 3 Kings indicate fraternities 2 Kings indicate business

XXI THE WORLD

LE MONDE

Conclusion

The production of the *Tarot Lovers' Tarot* deck and *"Little" Black Book of Tarot Card Meanings* has been a long, yet very rewarding journey. Therefore, we hope that you get many years of pleasure from using these cards and the insights that they contain.

For those of you who would like to know more about the fascinating world of Tarot, we have compiled the following short but very useful bibliography. For more information on *Tarot Lovers' Tarot* and additional *Tarot Lovers' Tarot* products, please visit: www.tarot-lovers.com or www.paranormality.com.

"Success is yours achieved at last, enjoy the attainments from your past."

Bibliography

Alexander, Skye. *The Only Tarot Book You'll Ever Need: Interpret the cards that hold your future.* (Adams Media, a division of FW+ Media, Inc. 57 Littlefield Street, Avon, MA 02322 USA, 2008).

Bartlett, Sarah. *The Tarot Bible: The Definitive Guide to the Cards and Spreads.* (Godsfield Press, a division of Octopus Publishing Group Ltd. 2-4 Heron Quays, London E14 4JP, 2006).

Connolly, Eileen. *Tarot: A New Handbook for the Apprentice* (Newcastle Publishing Company Inc. North Hollywood, California, 1979).

Dhingra, Guneeta. *All You Wanted to Know about Tarot.* (Sterling Publishers Pvt. Ltd. A-59 Okhla Industrial Area, Phase II, New Delhi 110020, 2000).

Douglas, Alfred. *The Tarot: The Origins, Meanings and Uses of the Cards.* (Penguin Books Inc, 7110 Ambassador Road, Baltimore, Maryland 21207 USA, 1973).

Doane, Doris Chase and King Keyes. *Tarot-Card Spread Reader* (Parker Publishing Company, Inc. West Nyack, NY, 1968).

Easton, Karyn. *The Tarot Lovers' Diary: Tarot Spreads, Tarot Card Meanings, Illustrations and Calendarial Information.* (Paranormality.com Publishers, 14 Nelson Road, Brixham, Devon TQ5 8BH, 2010).

Peach, Emily. *Discover Tarot: Understanding and Using Tarot Symbolism* (The Aquarian Press an Imprint of HarperCollinsPublishers, 77-85 Fulham Palace Road, Hammersmith, London W6 8JB, 1990).

Stuart, Rowenna. *Tarot: Find out Where your Future Lies.* (Harper Collins Publishers, Westerhill Road, Bishopbriggs, Glasgow G64 2QT, 1998).

Waite, Arthur Edward. *The Pictorial Key to the Tarot.* (Dover Publications Inc.; New edition, 26 Aug 2005).

Resources

www.aeclectic.net/tarot/

www.paranormality.com

www.tarot-lovers.com